Dr. Sa'eed of Iran

Dr. Sa'eed

The Life Story of

Dr. Sa'eed of Iran

KURDISH PHYSICIAN TO PRINCES AND
PEASANTS, NOBLES AND NOMADS

by

JAY M. RASOOLI

AND

CADY H. ALLEN

William Carey Library

PO Box 40129
Pasadena, California 91104

Second Edition, August, 1958
First William Carey Library Edition, July, 1983

ISBN 0-87808-743-5
Library of Congress Cataloging Number 57-13245

Published by
William Carey Library
1705 N. Sierra Bonita Ave.
PO Box 40129
Pasadena, California 91104

Cover Design, Frontispiece and sketch of Kaka on page 168 by Gene Keller.
Pen sketches by Dirk Gringhuis

Printed in the United States of America

DEDICATED

to

the memory of

KAKA RASOOLI

My beloved father, proud of lineage but humble of heart, gentlest of gentlemen, devoted father

J.M.R.

Esteemed colleague and faithful friend, eager evangelist and courageous soldier of the Cross

C.H.A.

PREFACE

Some friends who have seen parts of this book in manuscript have asked, "Is this all truth or partly fiction?" The answer is that every endeavor has been made to write only a true biography. Even when Dr. Sa'eed's thoughts or feelings have been described, the authority for them has come from the doctor himself, to whom I am indebted for most of the material gathered in preparation for this book. As his nephew, it was my privilege to live for six months in his home, observing at first hand his daily life and work and hearing from his own lips the account of many of his experiences. In addition, after I decided to write his biography, he furnished me with written answers to numerous questions and many other data that have made this book possible.

The first draft of this biography was completed fifteen years ago and was more than twice as long as the present book. For this drastic abridgment, made to comply with present-day trends in publication, I am indebted to the Rev. Cady H. Allen of New York City, who was for nearly half a century a missionary in Iran. His intimate knowledge of the country and long acquaintance with Dr. Sa'eed made it possible for him to undertake a thorough revision of my work, involving deletions, rearrangement of material, and some additions of his own, such as the resume of Avicenna's life, the summary of Dr. Sa'eed's outstanding characteristics, and numerous footnotes. For his collaboration and counsel I am deeply grateful.

I am further indebted to the late Mr. William R. Cox of Sussex, England, who through a long friendship with Dr. Sa'eed had collected material for a proposed biography, and to Mr. A.J. Pollock of Weston-Super-Mare, England, for placing these memoranda at my disposal; to the Misses Trench of Workington, Cumberland, England, and to Miss Mary Alexander of Washington, D.C. for other data; to Dr. Isaac Yonan's *The Beloved Physician of Teheran* (Cokesbury, 1934) for the account of the trip of his brother and Dr. Sa'eed from Urumia to Bijar; to Mr. Samuel Sade, the doctor's son, for other information and helpful suggestions; to others who have read the manuscript and have offered valuable criticisms; and to various standard books on Iran for historical references.

The King James translation of the Bible has been used for all quotations from Scripture, since it was the English version used by Dr. Sa'eed himself. Quotations from the Koran are from Rodwell's translation in *Everyman's Library*. No attempt has been made to be scientifically accurate in the transliteration of Persian words or names. It will be helpful for anyone who attempts to pronounce them to remember that the accent will fall on the last syllable and where the terminal vowel in that syllable is an *"i"*, it will be pronounced as *"ee"* in all proper names used in this book. *"Iran"* should be pronounced with *"i"* as in *"machine"* and *"a"* as in *"father."*

This biography is in no way interested in political affairs as such; any reference to historical events is merely to provide background for the narrative. The sole purpose of the book is to portray a life which has an abundance to offer in the way of guidance, encouragement, and inspiration, in the hope that it may bring genuine help of this kind to those who read it, even as its writing has brought me spiritual uplift.

Jay M. Rasooli, M.D.

October, 1957
San Pedro, California

8

CONTENTS

ILLUSTRATIONS

Introductory

Map of IRAN showing places visited by Dr. Sa'eed

INTRODUCTORY

A crescent-shaped mountainous region, covering areas in eastern Turkey, northern Iraq, and northwestern Iran,[1] bears the name of Kurdistan. It is not a geographical entity with definite boundaries nor a political state, but the homeland of the Kurds, an ethnic group of Aryan extraction come down from the remote past, retaining their racial purity, their distinct dialects, their characteristic customs. It is a land of wild grandeur and matchless beauty, with its awe-inspiring mountains lifting their snowclad peaks up to heaven, its deep ravines with their cascading torrents, and its green valleys lush with grass for springtime pasturage.

The million or so Kurds are for the most part either villagers living in small hamlets of mud-brick houses, around which they graze their sheep and cattle, or nomadic herdsmen, moving their black tents to warmer or cooler climes as the changing seasons demand. The few cities, none of them large, are centers of trade between these country folk and the outside world. Tribal chieftains and feudal landlords possess great power.

The Kurds are a virile people, long famed for their generous hospitality, their intense fanaticism, their

---

[1]"Iran" has been for centuries the name of the whole land of Persia in the language of the country, whereas "Persia" comes from Fars, a province in the south. In line with the rapid progress made during the reign of Reza Shah (1925-41) foreign countries were asked to use the name "Iran" as more fitting than one derived from a single province. Since, however, the country was known as Persia during most of Dr. Sa'eed's life, that name will often be used in this biography.

13

brigandage and warlike proclivities. The Kurdish costume — short coat, baggy trousers, heavy sashbelt, turban — is most picturesque, and when dagger, cartridge belts, and rifle are added to make up the warrior, most formidable.

Old Kurdish Costume

Ever since the Mohammedan conquest of the seventh century the Kurds have been Moslems of the Sunni or orthodox sect, whereas the people of Iran as a whole belong to the other large division of Islam, the Shiahs. The higher ecclesiastics have vied with the tribal chieftains in the exercise of authority.

The most important city of Kurdistan is Senneh (also written Sanandaj), roughly eighty miles northwest of Hamadan, the classic Ecbatana, which in turn is 240 miles from Teheran, the capital of Iran. This Kurdish town of 46,685 inhabitants,[2] with its well-built houses, busy bazaars, and surrounding gardens, lies snugly in a valley at an elevation of 5,300 feet. Its numerous mosques with minarets pointing skyward testify to its fanatical religious atmosphere.

---

[2] By the 1956 census. In Dr. Sa'eed's time the population was not so large.

14

Dr. Sa'eed of Iran

CHAPTER ONE

A Youth on a Spiritual Quest

It was the first day of June, 1863.[1] On the outskirts
of Senneh, in the tanners' quarter, two men were playing on reed pipes in the street and a third was beating
a drum, while men and women, alternating in a circle,
danced with laughter around the musicians. Presently
the solid wooden gate in the mud wall opened on its
creaking hinges and a smiling, white-turbaned mullah[2]
appeared, whereupon musicians and dancers redoubled
their exertions. Some one shouted, "God bless Mullah
Rasool and his family!" A large tray of raisins and
dried peas was brought out. The peas were roasted
over an open fire and the whole company partook of the
simple refreshments. On receiving a small present of

[1]1279 by the Mohammedan calendar, which dates from the Hegira,
or flight of Mohammed from Mecca to Medina.
[2]A mullah is a Mohammedan ecclesiastic.

17

money, the musicians departed and the group broke up.
Thus was celebrated in true Kurdish style the birth of
Mullah Rasool's baby boy. Had it been a girl, there
would have been no music and dancing, only disappointment.

When his guests had departed, Mullah Rasool stepped
back into the little courtyard with its high mud walls
and cobble-stone paving. He skirted the stone-lined
pool, where morning toilets were performed and dishes
were washed, and climbed the six or eight high steps to
the living quarters of the simple home. Slipping off
his shoes on the flagstoned porch, he returned to the
room where his wife was lying on her pallet with her
newborn child in its cradle beside her.

It was a modest house — three rooms side by side,
the middle one somewhat smaller and set back to allow
for a porch, with a basement underneath, level with the
ground, for stores and kitchen. The earthen floors were
covered with reed matting and carpeted with strips of
course felt or with *galims*.³ In wintertime the center of
the two side rooms was occupied by a *kursi*.⁴ Niches in
the walls held various objects — this one a few china
dishes and bric-a-brac; that one a samovar, a teapot, and
little glasses on a brass tray; and another the mullah's
miniature library of tall books with names pasted on
their black leather covers. In the main sitting room,
where the mullah received his men guests, the white-
washed walls were undecorated, save for a rifle hanging
from a peg and a dagger or two. The windows were
heavy wooden frames with small panes or here and
there a piece of paper to replace missing glass. During
the daytime bundles of bedding, set against the walls,

---

³A *galim* is a coarse woven carpet without pile.
⁴A *kursi* is a sort of low, square table placed over a depression in
the floor. Underneath is set a brazier of glowing charcoal. The
whole device is covered with a large, heavy quilt. The family sits
around this on mattresses, reclining against cushions or bundles of
bedding, with the quilt pulled up around their bodies. Meals are
served on the *kursi*. At night the backrests are removed and the
people lie down, covered by the quilt, their heads resting on pillows
outside.

served as backrests for the people as they sat cross-legged on the floor. Wooden chests in the corners contained changes of clothing and other necessities. At night a small oil lamp placed on a shelf sent its feeble rays of light into the room where the family was gathered. At time for retiring the bedding rolls were opened up and stretched out on the floor for sleeping. Life was simple in the extreme.

A few days after the birthday celebration a mullah was invited to officiate at the naming of the child. Taking the baby in his arms, he recited some words from the Koran in each ear, transferred a small portion of date from his own mouth to the boy's, and declared: "I name thee by the noble name of Mohammed Sa'eed." This simple ceremony was in imitation of their Prophet on the occasion of his naming of his grandson, Hasan. From this time on the child was called Sa'eed, an Arabic word meaning "happy" or "fortunate."

Mullah Rasool was descended from generations of well-known Moslem ecclesiastics. He was the seventh of this long line and fully worthy of his lineage. Left an orphan at an early age, he was employed by his uncle as a farmhand and nightwatchman over cultivated fields where bears and wild boar wrought much damage. Dissatisfied with this peasant life and thirsting for knowledge, he had fled from his uncle's home in Turkish Kurdistan and made his way with many an adventure to Senneh, where Moslem theologians congregated. At times he slept, homeless and hungry, on the gate seats of the theological school or strained his eyes under the feeble light of the lantern overhead to decipher some old manuscript. By such assiduous effort he attained the status of mullah, though not of high rank.

Rasool's genuine piety had won for him permission from the city elders to write prayers to be read for the sick and afflicted, and many were the people who flocked to him for help and so contributed their coins or gifts of food toward his support. He possessed an old manuscript on the art of healing. With the use of this he ventured to treat all sorts of diseases with prescriptions in which herbs and superstition were oddly compounded, yet which sometimes proved efficacious. Another of Rasool's privileges was to go to the cemetery after a burial and instruct the newly interred. Soon after interment, according to Moslem belief, two angels come to catechize the deceased as to their religious allegiance. Their answers determine their future destiny. It was to prepare them with the proper responses that Rasool gave the needed instruction.

Mullah Rasool married a worthy girl of his own people, Mahenessa by name. She proved to be a practical, hard-working woman, endowed with moral courage and religious fervor. As a mother, her discipline was severe, but effective. Being a mullah's wife, she took part in many religious functions among the women, and many friends came to her for discussion and consultation. To this congenial couple eight children were born, but one after another had died, till at the time of Sa'eed's birth only Kaka[5] was left, a boy of eight.

Early realizing that Sa'eed was a child of superior intelligence and aptitude, Mullah Rasool devoted every effort to his training, and no pupil could have been more eager to learn. Many were the tales of Mohammedan saints and heroes that this father told his children before they could read or write. When not yet five, Sa'eed could repeat from memory many chapters of the Koran. Each night before retiring, sitting on his heels, knees together in front, hands on knees, he squatted on the floor beside his father and recited the six essentials of the Islamic creed — belief in God, his angels, his books, his prophets, the day of judgment, and the predestination of good and evil.

Sa'eed's talents were so obvious that he was considered in danger of the "evil eye," unless protected by some

---

[5]His real name was Mohammed, but Sa'eed always called him Kaka, Kurdish for "brother." By this name he came to be known.

special charm carried on his person. Accordingly, his father wrote to Sheikh Osman, a famous leader of a powerful mystic order, and procured an appropriate prayer, which was sewed inside the lad's hat. A communication from this prominent ecclesiastic was regarded a great honor. One day on the street an older boy boasted of his father.

"My father is a greater man," replied Sa'eed defiantly.

"He is not," challenged the other. "My father knows all the big people in town."

Sa'eed doffed his hat and pointed to the little roll of paper inside. "See that? This prayer was written especially for me by Sheikh Osman at my father's request. I'll bet your father doesn't even know Sheikh Osman."

The other's eyes dilated as he looked at the charm. Then he suddenly snatched the hat and ran away. With hot tears of indignation rolling down his cheeks, Sa'eed invoked the holy sheikh to paralyze the thief, but in vain. He was gone, never to be seen again.

Before Sa'eed was six, he started going to the school for boys which his father had opened for teaching Persian and Arabic. Sometimes the classes were held in part of the mosque where Mullah Rasool led the daily prayers, sometimes in another public building. In the winter they met in a large room which not only had no sun, but its one latticed window, devoid of glass, was covered with paper made semitranslucent with castor oil. Heat came from charcoal fires which the boys made in their own braziers, the poisonous fumes fouling the air. Here twenty or thirty boys sat cross-legged for eight hours a day, each on his own rug or cushion, each swaying back and forth as he recited out loud the passage from the Koran or the Persian poem he sought to memorize. Their teacher was seated at the head of the room on his own mattress and called each pupil to him for his private recitation. It was in such a school that Sa'eed laid the foundation of his education.

Discipline was administered by bastinado.[6] One day Kaka, out of jealousy, unjustly accused his brother of some misdemeanor. To escape punishment Sa'eed dashed barefooted out into the snow, but Kaka captured him and helped to fasten his ankles, while his father applied the switch to the soles of his feet already numb with cold. Mullah Rasool showed no partiality to his favorite child.

Sa'eed made rapid progress in his studies. Quite often Mullah Rasool would set the boys to capping verses of poetry, each one dropping out of the game when he failed to respond with a line beginning with the required letter. How elated the teacher was to see his younger son vie with the oldest pupil and hold him at bay! On the other hand, Sa'eed's eager questions sometimes embarrassed his father, whose knowledge of the world beyond the bounds of Persia was strictly limited.

Sa'eed's joy was full when hand in hand he accompanied his father to the mosques and listened attentively to the mullah's conversations with his friends. Of these experiences he used to say: "What echoes rose from the depths of my heart when I heard Father speak of pious men such as Ghazali![7] How I longed some day to experience these things myself!" In this way the thirst for knowledge and the hunger for holiness were coupled together in deepening intensity. But Mullah Rasool did most for Sa'eed by personal example, the spontaneous expression of a deeply religious nature and an upright character, and that in an atmosphere of ignorance, intolerance, and low moral standards.

Outside of Senneh, near the cemetery, was a leper colony where lived poor wretches, disowned by their families and shunned by all others as unclean and even as already dead. Their one friend was Mullah Rasool, who went to visit them from time to time, fearless of

---

[6]The oriental punishment of beating an offender on the soles of his feet.

[7]Ghazali was Persia's most famous mystic.

contagion. When they saw him coming, they would rush to greet him, their gaunt and disfigured faces lighting up with smiles of welcome. They would flock around him and call him "father." It seemed to them as if their Prophet himself had descended among them to soothe their pains and allay their despair. When one of these outcasts died he did not hesitate to wash the loathsome body so that it might have the last rites necessary for a proper Moslem burial.

One day the mullah took his little son along on his visit to the lepers. The sight of this healthy child made the call doubly welcome. One of the inmates forthwith presented Sa'eed with a penknife and asked his wife to fry some eggs for him. He was loath to eat the food prepared, but his father, sensitive to the feeling of the kindly couple, said: "How nice! Take some, my boy." Sa'eed obeyed. When they had returned home, his mother rebuked her husband: "Do you mean to say you took the child into a leper's house and made him eat their food?" He only smiled and continued his visits to the colony. Such selfless service to these wretched creatures could not but have had a profound influence on the awakening lad.

One day a foreigner visited Senneh. "Why is the Ferangi[8] wearing that funny hat with a broad brim?" Sa'eed asked his mother, for Persian hats were brimless in those days.

"He is an unbeliever," she replied, "and they do not wish him to see the sky, which is the abode of God." By such an answer was aversion to non-Moslems instilled in the receptive mind.

There were in Senneh some sixty families of Assyrian Roman Catholics[9] and a colony of Jews.[10] Toward these

---

[8]European

[9]These were formerly Nestorians, but under the influence of priests had adopted the Roman Catholic faith.

[10]There were colonies of Jews in many Persian cities, very probably descendants of the Jews deported to Babylon at the time of the Captivity.

also there was inculcated in Sa'eed an attitude of intolerance. As a youngster he would sometimes on a Saturday be asked by a Jewish housewife into her home to put out the fire, which her law forbade her to touch on the sabbath. Or at times he might have an errand in a Christian home. On such occasions he would pass close to a shelf, with his elbow send a dish or two crashing down, and then blandly offer profuse apology for the accident! Another trick was to sit on the floor and beneath his long, loose mantle cut holes in their rugs with his knife. Such misdeeds, while inspired by bigotry, were done especially to earn merit with God by causing damage to an unbeliever or even to one of a rival Moslem sect.

While still a young boy, long before reaching the age of religious obligations, Sa'eed assumed the yoke of Islamic rites. He began to attend public prayers at the mosque and prayed with such fervor and absorption that he seldom heard his name when called. One day during Ramazan[11] he decided to fast. Despite parental advice he went to school without eating or drinking. On returning home in the afternoon he was faint with hunger. His mother urged him to take some soup she had prepared: "Eat, child. Fasting is not meant for one so young as you." The hour to break the fast had not yet arrived, but he took some of the soup, only to have his devout stomach eject it in rebellion!

One day in his ninth year he was performing his ablutions at the mosque, when a poor illiterate entered the courtyard and asked the mullah who was to lead the prayers to read a letter for him. The mullah examined it and then handed it back, saying, "It's so badly written I can't make it out." Sa'eed asked to see the letter and read it without difficulty. Amazed, the stranger turned to the mullah with his white turban, symbolic of learning, and said, "The child read it nicely and I understood it

---

[11]The month of fasting in Islam, when food and drink are forbidden from before sunrise until after sunset.

thoroughly." "The boy writes a miserable hand himself," retorted the mullah; "that's why he can read such wretched writing!"

Through constant study and scrupulous attention to ritual and worship, by the age of ten he had become the prodigy of Senneh. Already his mastery of Persian and Arabic classics, his knowledge of Islamic theology and traditions, had excited the admiration of his people. He devoted himself rigorously to the cause of Islam, no duty being too exacting, if only it would help him to achieve holiness. Having a good voice, he used to give the call to prayer from the roof of the mosque which he attended.

Being fond of poetry, he spent many hours a day reading Kurdish poetical works about Mohammed's life. He even attempted to write poetry in the same style. Realizing that many people did not understand the meaning of the prayers they had to repeat in Arabic, he began writing them out in Kurdish poetry, but the mullahs discouraged him, declaring that translation of the holy words was a sin.

Clouds now began to gather above the horizon of Sa'eed's sunny life. A famine was raging and cholera was dealing deathblows by the thousand. Daily a line of haggard fugitives plodded out of the city gates seeking refuge elsewhere. Mullah Rasool had a desperate struggle to provide his family with the barest necessities of life. The epidemic had frightened away most of his pupils, dwarfing his income. Many a day he would fast that his children might have enough to eat.

One day the good mullah happened upon a purse containing enough money to tide his family over the crisis. The temptation to keep it was great, but it remained untouched until the owner was found. At school it was his habit to slip under his cushion the small silver which his pupils brought for tuition. Driven by hunger, Sa'eed often filched a coin from this petty hoard and bought raisins or fruit to eat in secret.

To add to the family troubles, thieves broke into their house and plundered it. The little reserve of wheat and flour, the paltry savings of cash, Mullah Rasool's sheepskin cloak—all were stolen. As a result, it was decided that the father should take the two boys away to a healthier place till cholera and famine should subside, while the mother remained behind with her newborn babe. The unflinching manner in which she accepted this arrangement was characteristic of her brave spirit.

The decision made, Mullah Rasool and the boys departed, coming back the next spring, when famine and cholera were over. The nursing mother, weak from malaria, succumbed to an attack of erysipelas and died shortly after their return. The hapless babe soon followed her to the grave.

Mullah Rasool would have preferred to remain a widower, but consideration of the children's comfort induced him to marry again. So the home was reestablished, but of course no one could take for the children the place of their own mother.

Three years passed. Toward the middle of Ramazan (1876)[12] Mullah Rasool himself was stricken with fever. Day by day he grew weaker and it became evident that the end was near. A summons was sent to Kaka, called to a neighboring village to read the Koran at the grave of a relative. Sa'eed was quietly sobbing in the room adjoining that where his father lay. Mullah Rasool called him and asked what was the matter. Sa'eed made a brave effort to smile, but his chin was quivering. "I know why you were crying," said the mullah. "You were crying because I am going to die and you will be left an orphan." Then, calling him nearer and taking his hand, he added: "Dear child, if you pursue the path of wisdom, though I be dead, you will not be fatherless. But if you should seek the ways of the foolish, even though I were alive, you would be an orphan." These words were the father's parting counsel to his beloved child.

---

[12]1293 by the Mohammedan calendar.

Sa'eed now abandoned hope for his father's recovery and poured out his soul in a plea to God: "If my dear father must die, then grant, O Lord, that he may be taken during the month of Ramazan, in these blessed days when Ali[13] was martyred, when the portals of thy mercy are flung wide open and those who enter come not into judgment." His beloved father passed away on the 21st of Ramazan, the very day of Ali's martyrdom. Kaka arrived two hours after the end had come.

Word of Mullah Rasool's death spread rapidly and hundreds of people gathered quickly to share in the merit of bearing the bier to the cemetery, where he was buried beside his wife.[14] The same day two brothers of the Imam Jum'eh[15] officiated at a memorial service in the mosque. After eulogizing Mullah Rasool, the younger brother, calling attention to Sa'eed, declared: "This boy, though young, is fully qualified to be a schoolmaster. His knowledge of Persian and Arabic, the Koran and the traditions, is far superior to mine and equal to my brother's, the Imam Jum'eh. I pray you, therefore, overlook his age and let him take his father's place in teaching your children." The people unanimously agreed.

The next day, before a huge gathering in the mosque, this same sheikh with great ceremony bound a white turban around Sa'eed's head to signify that he was formally invested with the title of "mullah." Within forty-eight hours of his father's death this boy of thirteen was elevated to be teacher and mullah — an unprecedented honor for one so young.

Hardly three months passed when a well-to-do Assyrian Roman Catholic asked Mullah Sa'eed to tutor his son

---

[13]Ali was Mohammed's son-in-law and the fourth caliph.

[14]In the East burial follows soon after death. In Iran as the bier is carried to the grave, men on the streets or in the shops will rush out to take the place of the bearers, if only for a few steps, to attain merit before God.

[15]The leader of the prayers at the Friday Mosque. Friday is the Moslem day of communal worship.

in Persian. The teacher soon became fond of his pupil
and sought to win him to the faith of Islam. One night,
while he was in his pupil's home, the latter's uncle came
in drunk. Going to the cupboard, he took out a bottle of
arak, a liquor of strong alcoholic content used in Iran.
When he had swallowed a glassful, he threw the remaining drops in his nephew's face and one drop fell on
Sa'eed's clothes. With intoxicating liquor forbidden in
the Koran and hence regarded as unclean, nothing could
have been more odious and defiling to a pious young
Moslem. In his extreme vexation he gave vent to his
indignation in abusive language. The bewildered pupil
apologized for his uncle's conduct and brought water to
wash out the stain, but it could not remove Sa'eed's
deepened prejudice against Christianity.

Some nights later they asked him to stay for dinner.
He declined, but with true Persian hospitality they insisted. Rather than hurt their feelings and as a gesture
of good will after his outburst a few days before, he took
a tiny bit of chicken, even though he regarded their food
unclean. When he reached home and retired, his conscience would permit no rest till he rose and disgorged
that unhallowed tidbit!

Thus, Sa'eed's impressions of the first Christians he
had met so far, aware of their worldliness and ignorance
of the scripture but their use of alcoholic beverages, as
seen through the strictness of Islamic teaching and personal prejudice, in his own words "made Islam seem more
glorious before my eyes. Often I thanked God that He
had created me a Moslem, born in the true religion."
With such thoughts his indebtedness to his forefathers,
who had first adopted Islam, led him to repeat daily the
prayer for the dead, that its merit might accrue their
account.

In sounding the call to prayer day after day there was
a new ring of spiritual fervor. When Ramazan came,
he gave himself more assiduously than ever to devotion-

al exercises. Nightly he sang the Supplications[16] from the rooftop. While others slept during the daytime to ease the rigors of the fast and spent the night in feasting, he ate one meal in the evening and took just a sip of water at dawn. These duties he imposed on himself to amass extra merit for his dead parents and relatives, for in Islam each act of worship properly performed has its special credit.

Three years passed in this manner. The young mullah left no stone unturned in his quest for knowledge and holiness, but his search left him dissatisfied and restive. During this time a copy of the New Testament in Persian came into his hands through a pupil. He read it from mere curiosity, found much in it that was unintelligible, and cast it aside in disgust. He made appointments with Catholic priests, but discussions with them proved fruitless. He was more than ever convinced of the superiority of Islam. It was here that he must satisfy his spiritual longings, but it would demand greater self-denial and austerity. So he sought satisfaction during this period in a new venture.

There was in Senneh a branch of a widespread powerful order of dervishes known as Naqshbandis. Sa'eed had heard rumors of some of these mystics who, after forty days of fasting and meditation, had had wondrous visions. Thinking that perchance here he could attain that elusive perfection he craved, he applied for membership, was accepted and inititated. Their leader pointed to the right side of Sa'eed's breast saying, "That flesh that desires evil things"; then to the left, "That beating means Allah, and you must repeat 'Al-lah, Al-lah, Al-lah' to the pulsations of your heart to attain piety."

The sect held its sessions in a mosque each night after the evening prayers, sitting on the floor in a circle in silence, waiting for the leader to repeat two special chapters of the Koran, which the others recited after him. Then each one said over different prayers inaudibly an

---

[16]Prayers usually taken from the Koran or Traditions.

odd number of times, keeping count by passing pebbles from one hand to the other. After that followed a pause in which each member was to think over his sins. He imagines himself sick, dying, dead, wrapped in his shroud, borne to the cemetery on his bier, lowered in his grave, the last prayer said. The two angels of death come to catechize him. He fails to answer aright and pictures himself in the flames of hell.

These imaginings were so vivid that there were moanings and tears. Then the leader would bare the breast of some overwrought devotee and breathe a "holy breath" over his heart, whereupon he would have a vision of Paradise and break into songs of praise.

For three years Sa'eed met faithfully with these mystic dervishes, performing their arduous rites for a contentment of heart that ever eluded him.

CHAPTER TWO

The Quest Rewarded

During the second and third centuries of the modern era, Christianity had penetrated far to the east. It is reported that by 225 A.D. it had made its way from the mountains of Kurdistan to the Persian Gulf. This "Church of the East" later became known as the Nestorian Church. Violent persecutions by the Zoroastrians in the fourth and fifth centuries scattered some of these Christians still farther afield—to Arabia, Turkestan and India. By the seventh century Nestorian missionaries had reached China. Then came the Moslem conquests and the Mongol invasions, which reduced this widespread church to two communities, one in southern India and the other among the Assyrian people, who lived in northwest Iran and over the border in Turkey.

In 1835 the first permanent Protestant missionary work in Iran was started in Urumia,[1] the chief center of the

---

[1]Now Rezaieh, so named after Reza Shah. The first missionaries were from the American Congregational Church, but in 1871 the work was turned over to the Presbyterians (U.S.A.) and has since been continued by them in the northern half of Iran.

Assyrian nation, a city in the northwest corner of the country. It was not the intention of the early missionaries to start a Protestant movement, but, if possible, to revive the Nestorian Church, which had sunk into lifeless formalism, and to reawaken its ancient evangelistic zeal. In this they were disappointed. The new wine was too strong for the old wineskins. Opposition arose and after some twenty years of labor they felt they had no choice but to separate and organize a Protestant Church. The project flourished: churches and schools sprang up in the surrounding villages all over the Urumia plain, teachers and doctors were trained, and dedicated Christian evangelists carried the message of the Gospel to distant centers in Iran.

On a late autumn day in 1879, when Mullah Sa'eed was in his seventeenth year, three of these devoted laborers, mounted on their animals, could be seen wending their way into Senneh. They were a pastor, Yohanan (Syriac for John), and two colporteurs, educated and trained in Urumia, come to propagate their faith in this fanatical town. Kasha[2] Yohanan was staying in Senneh for some time and so needed a more fluent use of Persian, which was not the vernacular of his province. In response to his inquiries for a tutor, Mullah Sa'eed was recommended.

The young teacher had heard his Catholic acquaintances speak of Protestants as heretics. If, then, he looked down upon orthodox Christianity as far inferior to Islam, to what an infinite degree must a faithful Moslem surpass these Christian dissenters! So it was with all the dignity of his position and a deep consciousness of superiority that Mullah Sa'eed knocked at Kasha Yohanan's door. Judging, as some strict Mohammedans do, that it was unlawful for a true Moslem to give an unbeliever the customary salutation, *"salamun alaikum"* (Peace be with you), he greeted the newcomers with a simple "Good morning." Quick to perceive the implication, one of the

---

[2] "Kasha" is the title of an ordained minister in Syriac.

colporteurs said: "But we are 'people of the Book'[3] and it is lawful to wish us peace." This unusual reply astonished the young mullah: these Christians were conversant with Koranic teaching!

He was now perplexed as to what greeting to use the next day. He did not wish to offend these people, yet his prejudice would not permit him to use the salutation of peace. His clever brain evolved a saving device. So he hailed the trio with "*sehamun alaikum,*" uttered quickly in the hope that the difference of a single Arabic letter would not be detected. Translated, it means, "May arrows strike you!"

One day Sa'eed arrived at Kasha Yohanan's at the time of their morning devotions. He was invited to join them and given a copy of the Psalms to follow as they read in turn. Then one of the Christians prayed in Persian. The feature of the prayer that especially impressed Sa'eed was a petition for God's blessing on friends and enemies alike. Had he not often been hired to write prayers for people for the destruction of their enemies?

Sa'eed began to apply the unfailing touchstone of works against words. He watched the trio closely day by day and became convinced that the accusations brought against Christians were groundless in their case. They never drank. They were truthful in speech and honest in their dealings. They never spoke evil of their neighbors. What they professed and practised agreed. Sa'eed began to like them. All Christians were not as bad as he was wont to think!

In course of time the two colporteurs left for Baghdad and Kasha Yohanan settled down to his new task. He was a man of forty, slenderly built, with a kind, dreamy face that bespoke an idealist. His absolute simplicity and sincerity attracted his young teacher. From language study conversation turned frequently to religion. Now that there was no longer a feeling of estrangement be-

---

[3]"People of the Book" is an expression often used in the Koran of Jews and Christians.

tween them, Sa'eed often volunteered the questions
closest to his heart. He had been taught the common
Moslem belief that the Bible in its present form was a
corrupted version of the "Books" Mohammed proclaimed
as divinely inspired. His first concern was its authenticity. So he began to study modern and ancient Syriac with
his pupil that he might compare the various translations.

Kasha Yohanan gave him a New Testament in modern
Syriac and taught him a few verses from the Gospel of
John. At home he showed the book to Kaka, detailing
what had happened between himself and the pastor. Kaka
was angry: "The evil effects of these books are beyond
number. Who knows but they will lead you astray?"
He warned Sa'eed that he was playing with fire and
urged him to concentrate on the advanced study of Islamic law and theology that he was pursuing under a
learned scholar. However this did not deter Sa'eed, but
merely convinced him that he must undertake his hazardous investigations without Kaka's knowledge.

In addition to their discussion of many points, as Christian and Moslem employed the Bible as their textbook for
the study of Persian, Kasha Yohanan had frequent arguments with Jews. On these occasions he asked Sa'eed
to act as referee by looking up pertinent passages in the
Bible. The Christian pastor cited many verses to prove
that Jesus was the promised Messiah. The Jews remained
adamant, but the impartial young judge was influenced
without realizing it. His sympathies were with the pastor
and he reproached the Jews for rejecting proofs they
could not refute.

When by himself, Sa'eed would ponder the prophecies
concerning the Messiah. Who could be worthy of such
wonderful predictions but Mohammed? Yet how could
the character portrayed in Isaiah 42:1-3, for example, be
the Prophet of Islam? "Behold my servant, whom I up-
hold; mine elect, in whom my soul delighteth; I have
put my spirit upon him. . . He shall not cry . . . nor cause
his voice to be heard in the street. A bruised reed shall

he not break, and the smoking flax shall he not quench." Islam had been spread by the power of the sword. Mohammed had in person led his followers to battle. Such things did not correspond with the prophecies of Isaiah.

After some time Sa'eed ventured to take a Bible home and show it to Kaka. He told him of the marvelous prophecies which he still believed must in some way refer to Mohammed. He begged of his older brother, who now had the authority of the household in place of his father, that he might continue his Syriac studies so that he could write a refutation of Christianity. This pleased Kaka and other friends who recognized the young mullah's scholarly proclivities. So permission was given. From now on Sa'eed studied the Bible openly.

As he pursued his study, he exercised great caution to accept nothing without careful reflection. At the same time his watchful eye was upon the life of the pastor to find aught that might not harmonize with his teaching. For him this was the decisive test. Later on Sa'eed wrote:

"From day to day I found myself more drawn to the pastor. His love, his truthfulness, his pious life, his meekness, and his honesty affected me deeply. I used to listen to his conversations with as many as came to him. I weighed every bit of it in the balance of reason. I could see how true his points were and how weighty his arguments, but above all, his life was a decisive witness to what he said."

It was the influence of this Christian character that introduced a change in Mullah Sa'eed's spiritual outlook. For the first time he became aware of the magnitude of his own shortcomings.

Over and over he spoke to the pastor about sin, repentance and salvation, seeking to understand the Christian teaching. With respect to "clean" and "unclean" he used the illustration of blood: "If there were but a single drop of it on our clothes, our prayers would be void, because blood is unclean."

"Then what about the blood that courses through your whole body?" the pastor asked.

"That is inside us, and since we judge the outward state, that does not matter."

"But in prayer the Christian is not concerned with the exterior, for true prayer proceeds to God from the heart and is not affected by the outward condition."

By such conversations Kasha Yohanan shattered Sa'eed's fallacies. After two or three months of similar discussions the young mullah began to have doubts. Hitherto he had never questioned his own religion or the faith of his forefathers. But now he had no peace of mind. As he himself testified, the pastor's words were ever present with him: they haunted his mind in the streets; they followed him to the market place; even during his prayers they never left him. His heart had no respite from their assaults. He berated himself a thousand times for associating with this Christian and through converse with him allowing these fiendish thoughts to pierce the armor of his mind. Would that he had heeded the admonition of his holy book: "O ye who have believed! form not intimacies among others than yourselves. They will not fail to corrupt you."[4] He searched his books diligently for some balm to soothe his lacerated breast, but in vain.

One day he was passing through a quiet, narrow street on his way to evening prayers. All of a sudden the thought burst unwanted upon him, "What if, after all, Mohammed were not a true prophet?" For a moment he was dazed with the shock of such a blasphemous suspicion. Then with clenched fists he began to beat his head, calling himself unclean and accursed. "O, why should my mind give birth to so vile a doubt?" he moaned in anguish. He kept saying to himself that Islam was the only true way, but still lurking uncertainty persisted.

He reflected on the pastor's life. How was it possible for an unbeliever to be so virtuous a man? Then the true

---
[4]Sura 3:114

picture of his inner self, stripped of all its punctilious piety, flashed on his mind like a hideous phantom, ugly and repulsive. He shuddered. He remembered the words of his Prophet: "Ye are the best folk that hath been raised up unto mankind."[5] As he contrasted his life with that of Kasha Yohanan, this assertion did not accord with the facts and only added to his dismay. On reaching the mosque, he hastened to his ablutions to wash away the pollution he had encountered, but he returned home with a heavy heart.

That night he had no appetite. He retired early, but he could not sleep. He groaned and sighed, tossed and sighed again. Finally, he arose, firmly resolved to settle once and for all this tormenting question. He lighted a fire and from the glowing embers took a live coal in the tongs and pressed it against one leg and then another coal against the other leg. He could hear the sizzle of burning flesh. He suffered excruciating pain, but he held on unflinchingly until two deep wounds were formed. It took them a long time to heal, leaving two permanent scars. This was according to Kurdish practice: when a Kurd makes a vow, he makes a scar on his body as a perpetual reminder to keep him faithful. So one of Sa'eed's scars was to remind him of the vow he had just made, never henceforth to speak with Christians about religion. The other was to bring to mind his shameful conduct and help him to avoid evil.

He now sent word to Kasha Yohanan that increasing duties would no longer permit him to teach after school hours and that he must forego further study of Syriac. "But as time went on," he later wrote, "I soon discovered that, though the burns on my body were healed, the wounds which the words of this man of God had produced in my mind were not. The burning within me was like a flame of fire. I was brought to the sad realization that all my diligence in attempting to make my ways and

[5]Sura 3:106

works better was of no avail. The more I tried, the worse things became."

Meanwhile Kasha Yohanan, aware of Sa'eed's spiritual struggles and fervently praying for him, made several attempts to see him. On these occasions he sought to drop some remark or quote some Bible verse to keep burning the flame that had been kindled.

One night, returning from prayers at the mosque, Sa'eed reached the covered passage leading to his gateway. There, alone by himself, he fell on his face in the dust of a dark corner and gave full vent to his pent-up misery in bitter tears. From the depths of his distraught soul he sobbed out his passionate prayer: "O Guide of Wanderers, lead me in the true way which is according to thy will. Take away the veil and give comfort to my heart. Deliver me, deliver me I plead, from this deadly whirlpool and grant me to serve thee as is worthy of thyself."

Even as he uttered these words a weight seemed to be lifted. He arose, resolved to investigate diligently both Bible and Koran and to delve into the life history of his Prophet. This meant that he was ready to study again with Kasha Yohanan.

For some four or five months he pursued this earnest course with all avidity. In both Bible and Koran he found numerous difficulties. Through the pastor's explanations his perplexities about Bible teachings were solved to his satisfaction. He found the fulfilment of Old Testament prophecies and hopes in the sinless Christ and came to understand that in salvation from sin there was peace of heart — a peace not yet his. The Koran he studied with the aid of the best commentaries, but many difficulties he encountered remained unsolved. In spiritual quality he found it much inferior to the Bible. He afterward wrote: "In Mohammed's teachings and personal life I found nothing which would satisfy the longing soul — not a drop of water to quench the thirsty spirit."

Without fully realizing the reason, he became increasing attached to Kasha Yohanan and almost a stranger to his own kin, even to his brother. This situation brought to his mind a couplet from Saadi: [6]

Much dearer one stranger who Godward doth lead
Than a thousand of kinsfolk without any creed.

With this growing friendship he spent more time at the pastor's house in study and discussion.

Kaka, now suspicious of his brother's moods and movements, reproved him with cutting words. He boasted of his own Prophet and spoke sarcastically of Christian "infidels." One day in anger he even broke several sticks to pieces on his brother's head and arms. Sa'eed fell on his face and kissed the ground at Kaka's feet. When Kaka left, he lifted his heart to God where he lay: "O merciful God! In thy presence I am less than the dust in which I lie — a helpless sinner in need of thy pity. Let my tears of penitence move thy heart of love. I beg for mercy, though deserving only judgment. Wash me, cleanse me, and receive me for the sake of thy Son."

On a perfect fall day not long after this experience Sa'eed was seated in the pastor's room. Kasha Yohanan had been in Senneh for nearly a year now and was planning to leave soon to return home. Sa'eed's mind was filled with sadness at the impending departure, when of a sudden there rang in his heart like the glad peal of a carillon the stirring call of Isaiah to captive Israel: "Arise, shine; for thy light is come, and the glory of the Lord is risen upon thee." [7] These words echoed and reechoed within him until every fiber of his being throbbed to the joyous call. As he gazed out of the window, the day glowed with a new beauty because of his inward joy.

"Arise, shine . . . For, behold, the darkness shall cover the earth, and gross darkness the people; but the Lord shall arise upon thee, and his glory shall be seen upon

---

[6]Saadi was a famous Persian poet of the 13th century.
[7]Is. 60:1

thee."⁸ Thus the refrain rang again and again. The power
of the words overwhelmed him. This was ecstasy indeed
after the months of doubt and bewilderment. All unknown to him, his inward rapture was mirrored in his
face. Kasha Yohanan perceived the transformation and
gently asked the cause. When Sa'eed had told of his new
joy, they both knelt and thanked God. "My dear boy,"
said the pastor, "rejoice, for you have found grace with
God."

The long and toilsome quest had attained its goal. The
pilgrim had arrived at home.

---

⁸Is. 60:1-2

CHAPTER THREE

Tested

After a few glad days of intimate Christian fellowship the sad hour of Kasha Yohanan's departure arrived. As a parting gift he gave Sa'eed a Persian and a Syriac New Testament. His farewell words were both encouragement and warning: "My dear boy, out of the thousands of people in this town of darkness God has chosen you alone as the object of his mercy and led you to your Savior. The light of Christ has indeed risen upon you. Therefore, be diligent in prayer that you may be kept from temptation. You may say to yourself, 'My learned ancestors knew better than I. I had better follow in their footsteps.' If you do, your end will be worse than your beginning." These words never lost their ring through the years.

As Kasha Yohanan set out on his journey home, Sa'eed accompanied him only a short distance for fear of being seen with him. When the pastor's kind face turned toward him for the last time, he was seized with a sense of utter loneliness. He sighed as he turned back: "I am left all alone. What shall I do with Kaka?" A child in the street was mercilessly beating a helpless puppy with a stick. The little creature was whining pitifully. The incident changed into a parable: he was the little dog and Kaka the boy. "No," he thought, "the time is not ripe to tell Kaka anything."

He was now confronted with a tormenting dilemma. Confession of his new faith was to court death. Flight, though tempting to contemplate, was difficult to achieve. And so began a double life of dissimulation and consequent torture of conscience. He attended the mosque less frequently, but because of his established position, he was charged with giving the call to prayer. When the call is sounded, the *muezzin*[1] pauses after each sentence and repeats it quietly to himself. After intoning the words, "I testify that Mohammed is the apostle of God," he would pray softly, "O God, forgive me." He hoped the Lord would recognize the mitigating circumstances and pardon him.

The call finished, he would linger on the rooftop so that some one else might lead the prayers. Then he would go down and take his place among the people, but instead of repeating the prescribed words as he bowed and prostrated himself, he would whisper the Lord's Prayer and the Apostles' Creed, emphasizing the sibilant sounds *s* and *sh,* which occur frequently in the Moslem ritual. In private he would say the Lord's Prayer and the Apostles' Creed thirty times, counting them over on the joints of his fingers as the Naqshbandis sometimes did, thinking such exercises a means of developing piety.

Later on he learned that Catholics abstained from meat on Fridays. Not to be outdone, he would eat nothing at all on that day. As for the fast of Ramazan, he kept it in public, but in private he would eat in some solitary retreat. Thereafter, these secret nooks that had witnessed

---

[1]One who gives the call to prayer.

his dissimulations would silently accuse him as he passed them, harassing his restive conscience till he would creep there to make atonement by tears of repentance, crying out, "O God, deliver me from this heartbreaking life."

Some weeks passed thus. At last the glowing fire in his breast compelled him to speak out. Among his companions were two or three with whom he was especially intimate. One of these was Faizullah, a wise and kind friend. One Friday on the roof of the principal mosque, where Sa'eed now lingered till the prayers were over, he revealed his secret to his comrade. What a joy to open his pent-up heart after all these days of lonely misery! Day after day they talked together of Sa'eed's new-found faith, Faizullah seeking to win him back to Islam.

Persuasion having failed, Faizullah tried to cheer his friend by diversion. One day he invited Sa'eed with a select group of companions to his father's country place. While the samovar was heating for tea, the young men were singing and clapping their hands, but Sa'eed's heart was not in the merriment. Taking some bread, he walked out into the vineyard, where he knelt down and poured out his heart in prayer. Eating the bread with some grapes plucked from a vine, he meditated on the death of Christ. It was in very truth his first Lord's Supper.

Encouraged by speaking to Faizullah, Sa'eed next approached Habib, his childhood playmate and neighbor. It was the month of Ramazan and Habib was fasting. They strolled into the country and sat down by a brook. Sa'eed stooped down and took a drink. Habib was horrified and exclaimed: "Are you crazy? Have you forgotten you are fasting?" Briefly Sa'eed told him of his new faith, warning that a breach of this confidence would endanger his life. With deep concern and pity Habib bemoaned the lapse of his bosom friend. After that they had many talks together, till Habib's heart was touched.

The circle of Sa'eed's confidants was gradually widening. So long as these were his close friends, there was little actual risk, for none of them wished to expose him.

The danger came from another quarter. A Jewish practitioner, hearing that Sa'eed knew Syriac, asked him if he would like to learn Hebrew also. Since he was glad to have this opportunity, it was arranged that the doctor should teach him Hebrew and he the children of the family Persian. The doctor had many friends whom Sa'eed engaged in religious discussion. To answer their questions he was obliged to study many portions of the Old Testament. To be refuted out of their own books by a Kurd so enraged them that in revenge they broadcast the word, "Your mullah has turned Christian."

Gossip spread. On the streets Sa'eed heard people say, "There goes the accursed fellow!" Some reviled him openly. He was reminded of the Persian proverb, "There is balm for the gash of an arrow, but wounds of the tongue nothing can heal." With none to sympathize, he often sought some sequestered spot where he might be alone.

In these days a Catholic merchant, Fattah by name, returned from Russia to Senneh. He was a God-fearing, broad-minded man, familiar with the Bible. Since he knew Kasha Yohanan, Sa'eed called on him. Gradually the conversation turned to their common friend. When they were alone, Fattah ventured to ask, "Did you receive any light through him?" Sa'eed at once unburdened his heart. Fattah rejoiced at the news, but asked: "Have you considered all the difficulties and dangers involved in this decision? Are you willing to give up your own people and the honor you have among them and, if necessary, leave your home? If not, you had better keep away from Christianity."

Sa'eed was deeply moved by this solemn warning. He replied: "Neither honor among my people, nor the benefits of this world, nor even loss of life, can make me forsake Christ, my Savior and my Guide to eternal life."

The good merchant's heart rejoiced at this confession. "Then I have brought you a present which will serve you well. Take these books and read them with care." He handed Sa'eed several volumes, including translations of Pfander's[2] works. Sa'eed received them gladly, but had to hide them carefully, lest their discovery by Kaka cause further trouble. Several kind Catholics offered him the freedom of their homes, where he could study in peace. Of these opportunities he availed himself freely.

As yet Sa'eed had made no confession to his brother, but from the changes in his home life Kaka realized that some decisive step had been taken, for Sa'eed no longer read his Koran in the mornings nor said his prayers. Now by sarcasm, now by boasts of Mohammed and by disparaging remarks about "Christian dogs," often by threats or thrashings, Kaka and other friends tried to force Sa'eed to revive his former practices. Once they persuaded him to visit the leader of the Naqshbandis,[3] a man who had undergone the forty days of fasting and was thought to fathom the secrets of men's hearts. After some conversation he addressed Sa'eed in a harsh tone: "Through your acquaintance with unbelievers you have a thick cloud of darkness over your heart. Beware! Shun the company of infidel dogs or you will surely be led astray."

As troubles multiplied and danger to life increased, Sa'eed attempted to escape from Senneh, but his plans were discovered and thwarted. He was frequently tempted to renounce his Christian faith, but consideration of the spiritual consequences deterred him. Burdened with the needs of his people, he wrote several letters to Kasha Yohanan and the American Mission in Urumia, but no answer came.

One day the Imam Jum'eh[4] sent for Sa'eed: "I want to know something about the Christian religion. Bring me a Bible and show me some passages with which you are acquainted." Sa'eed took him his Persian New Testa-

---

[2]Pfander was a German missionary and scholar who had spent a short time in Iran and who had written books in refutation of Islam, the most famous of which is *The Balance of Truth.*

[3]See page 29.

[4]Leader of prayers at the Friday Mosque.

ment and called attention to certain places. On a later visit the Imam Jum'eh said, "I find nothing in this book to justify hatred of Christians by Moslems." Sa'eed was delighted, but then made a mistake which he at once regretted. Instead of letting the Word of God speak for itself, he gave the man his copy of Pfander's *Balance of Truth,* a powerful polemic against Islam. It aroused the Imam Jum'eh's anger and he determined to write a refutation. Some days later he announced in the principal mosque that His Majesty the King had sent him this book, requesting him to write an answer!

Despite his yearning for eminence, the Imam Jum'eh was a kindly man. On more than one occasion he quelled the fury of the fanatics against Sa'eed, even though the Governor and the people were against him. Once when such a group came to ask him for a written decree sanctioning Sa'eed's death, he drove them from his house in anger.

In these days there came to Senneh an illustrious Catholic bishop, Mar Shimmon. He was a man eighty years old, simple, humble, well versed in the Bible. Sa'eed was quickly drawn to him, but it was not easy to visit him for fear of discovery. Sometimes he entered by the rear door of the church compound, occasionally he climbed over the back wall, at other times he ventured to go in by the front gate. Many were the hours that he read the Bible to the bishop in Arabic or Syriac. Many were the helpful teachings which this venerable saint gave the young convert.

The companionship thus established, however, was soon to end. On one of his customary visits Sa'eed found his friend packing to leave. The bishop had heard that the British Consul General had started for Mosul (Mar Shimmon's native city) and he was anxious to overtake him to travel with the protection his official position would afford. Once again Sa'eed resolved on flight. The morning after the bishop left he set out on foot with no provisions and the equivalent of only twenty-five cents in money, hoping to catch up with him. He walked for ten miles, but in vain, for the bishop had traveled in haste by night. Discouraged and hungry, he plodded his weary way back with feet so blistered that for days he walked with a limp.

Winter now set in. With the bishop gone his loneliness was greater than ever. Persecution at home had become almost unbearable. Kaka's caustic remarks taxed Sa'eed's endurance to the limit. As they were seated one day around the *kursi*, Sa'eed was reading to a neighbor from a Moslem book about Mohammed's birth and the marvelous signs that accompanied it, such as the appearance to his mother of Eve, Sarah, the Virgin Mary, and the angel Gabriel, to minister to her, while Satan and his hosts were grievously lamenting, because the event betokened the destruction of their works.

Kaka began to boast about such a wonderful prophet, but Sa'eed ventured to question the authenticity of the narrative and to suggest that they investigate the "heavenly sources" (i.e., the Bible) to see if they could find anything about the coming of Mohammed. To this the neighbor agreed, but Kaka was furious. He lifted his hand to the loaded gun hanging on the wall and aimed it at his brother. Sa'eed did not move, but the neighbor threw himself on the gun and wrenched it from Kaka's hands.

It was now amply clear to Sa'eed that naught but persecution and danger remained for him in Senneh. What could he do? Kaka was engaged to be married: if the wedding could be hastened, perchance his thoughts could be diverted from his brother to his bride. But Kaka refused to be hurried. Another possibility was flight, but two attempts at escape had been foiled. One other course remained, but it involved grave risk — to come out with the whole truth. It was not that Kaka was unaware of what was going on, but that he pretended not to recognize the reality of his brother's conversion.

Sa'eed weighed the matter carefully. He remembered full well the Koranic injunction to kill apostates[5] and he was sure this would be his fate, brought about by his own brother's hand. For a long time he had been facing death daily. He thought of the Persian proverb, "There is no color beyond black." He finally decided to make a full confession to Kaka, not by word of mouth, for that would at once bring on a spasm of fury, but in writing.

As if penning a farewell letter to his brother, he wrote:

"Glory to the only wise and invisible God, who will honor those who lay down their lives for him . . . For me to remain longer in this town is impossible. When you are acquainted with my views, if you will kill me, I shall count myself a martyr, for I am sure of God's acceptance. Should you spare me, as long as I live I shall be your servant. Do not ask me for proofs while you are angry. . . . . I have been a Christian now for some time . . . . You know what people think about me. To remain longer in this town is full of danger for me. . . ."

Sa'eed had written his own death warrant. For days he carried this bit of dynamite in his bosom, wavering between fear and hope.

One night when the two brothers and a neighbor were sitting around the *kursi*, the conversation turned to religion. Kaka and the visitor made cutting remarks unbearable to Sa'eed. Stepping outside, he knelt on the frozen ground for a moment of prayer, seeking help in this time of crisis. Then he went in, took out the letter, and handed it to his brother. From Kaka's change of color and shaking hands the neighbor guessed the nature of the contents and hurriedly excused himself.

Both brothers were trembling with suspense. When Kaka reached the sentence requesting him to demand no proofs until his anger had subsided, he held the letter to the flame of the oil lamp and burned it. Fortunate for Sa'eed, that this written proof of his apostasy was destroyed!

---

[5]Sura 4:90-91

They both lay down for the night in the warmth of the *kursi*, but neither could sleep, the one from towering rage, the other from fear. At last Kaka began to speak, and with each sentence his indignation rose. Sa'eed's silence only stirred his passion to a higher pitch. Finally, he shouted: "A dog[6] and a man cannot live together. Clear out!"

Their house being near the edge of the city, in winter after dark wolves sometimes came near in search of food. "Where can I go on a night like this?" pleaded Sa'eed.

"What has that got to do with me?"

"Please let me stay in tonight. Tomorrow I will go."

"Get out, accursed dog!" Kaka raised his hand to the gun.

Hastily Sa'eed put on his clothes and went out into the dark and bitter cold. Wandering aimlessly, thinking of the persecution of his followers foretold by Christ, he knocked at the doors of his Catholic friends, but from fear of entertaining this apostate they offered excuses. He could not blame them. Finally, an old woman for whom he had often written letters took him in and gave him a warm bed. To save her from the obloquy of having kept the apostate in her home, he left early so as not to be seen and went to the school, there to be ready for his pupils and for whatever God had in store.

Meanwhile Kaka rose early also, took his gun and stationed himself in a shop opposite the Catholic church, where he supposed Sa'eed had probably taken refuge. When asked what he was doing there with a gun, he replied: "My brother has become an infidel. I am waiting here to kill him."

When people now saw Sa'eed's only brother hunting him with a gun and testifying to his apostasy, they cast aside all reserve and began to plot his destruction. Whereas Kaka was ready to kill Sa'eed himself, he was not ready to turn him over to a fanatical mob. He now began to feel pity for his brother. Hastily he sought the advice

---

[6]Dogs are considered unclean by strict Mohammedans.

of his stepmother's sister, a wise and good woman. Together they hurried to the school, where she effected a sort of reconciliation. Sa'eed was now received back into the home and as a Christian. Though reasonably safe in the house, Sa'eed dared not venture out at night for fear of a sudden assault. Faizullah, Habib, and other friends brought him news of the latest plots and warned him to avoid this and that trap.

When spring came (1881), three Protestant Christians from Hamadan came to Senneh for evangelistic work in response to Sa'eed's repeated appeals — Rev. James W. Hawkes, a newly arrived American missionary; Mirza Hovhannes, a leading Protestant Armenian; and Agha Hyeem, a converted Jew. They found the environment hostile. Unfortunately, they had with them an Armenian servant who stole some coins and antiques that Agha Hyeem had collected. When the Governor extracted a confession of the theft, the report spread like wildfire through the town that these Christians who had come to convert the Mohammedans were themselves thieves! Antagonism rose to fever heat.

It was also noised abroad that Sa'eed had given the Christians a Koran—an act of sacrilege to Moslems—and that he was to have his right hand cut off in public. A maddened mob went to the lodgings of the Christians to seize the desecrater. Providentially, the Imam Jum'eh's brother was calling there and dispersed the rabble. He also escorted Sa'eed to his home. After this untoward episode the visiting trio returned to Hamadan.

Mr. Hawkes, now fully awakened to the dangers that Sa'eed was daily facing, wrote him an invitation to come to Hamadan as his language teacher, since his former instructor had suddenly died. Sa'eed consulted Kaka: "My return to Islam is impossible. My stay here will mean death. Have pity and let me go." After consultation with a relative Kaka consented.

Absolute caution was necessary. It was arranged that Kaka should see his brother off to join a caravan outside of town. In midafternoon each left the house by a different route to meet at a certain crossroads, Kaka carrying his brother's few belongings—a small rug, saddlebag, change of clothes, and some books. Sa'eed marveled that Kaka had not only permitted him to go, but was actually furthering his escape.

When the pair, now joined, reached a brook, they found it swollen with the heavy spring rains. Deeming it inadvisable to use the bridge because of the danger of meeting traffic, they walked along the banks till they found a possible fording place. Kaka tucked up his trousers, removed his shoes, lifted Sa'eed with his bundle to his shoulders, and with difficulty crossed the dashing current. Years afterward Sa'eed wrote: "With this one act of kindness he poured a healing ointment into all the wounds he had inflicted before, the remembrance of which even now fills me with a strong emotion and brings tears to my eyes."

They reached the caravan at sundown. Sa'eed kissed Kaka's hand in deferential farewell and wept. Kaka left without a word. The caravan moved on about midnight and the young fugitive, sometimes riding, more often on foot, pushed forward till after sunrise, when the animals were halted to rest and feed. As they started on again, Sa'eed began to feel more secure. Suddenly his peaceful dream turned into a nightmare: there were Kaka, his friend Habib, and Allah Karam, a relative! They had come hotfoot to take him back. Sa'eed was petrified with fear.

Kaka called him aside: "The whole city is in an uproar. They have been to the Governor and demand your return. They threaten to tear down our house over my head. Have pity on me! Let us go back and ask protection. Return to Islam for your safety and mine." Habib and Allah Karam joined in the plea.

As they persisted, Sa'eed felt death inevitable. "Kill me here yourselves, for my return is impossible, my recantation unthinkable." Kaka was deeply moved. Habib was tugging at his arm. Sa'eed threw himself at Kaka's feet. "Kill me now," he implored.

In a last attempt Kaka took up Sa'eed's bag and walked off with his treasured books. Sa'eed followed, bent down, and kissed the hem of his brother's garment. "Take them all, but give me back my Bible!" Refused, he turned back. When Kaka realized that this final device had failed, he put the bag down and gave his brother a fond embrace. Then he turned with his two companions and walked away without a backward look. Sa'eed covered his face from the men of the caravan and wept bitterly.

When he was himself again, he began to think: "You have sent your brother away with a broken heart. Who knows what will befall him at the hands of those fanatics? And what will happen to you in Hamadan, a complete stranger? Say goodbye to Christianity and be at peace." Then there came to him, as if a voice were speaking, the words of his beloved Gospel: "If any man come to me, and hate not. . . his brethren, . . . yea, and his own life also, he cannot be my disciple."[7] "There is no man that hath left house or brethren, or sisters, or father, or mother, or wife, or children, or lands, for my sake, and the gospel's, but he shall receive an hundredfold now in this time . . . with persecutions; and in the world to come eternal life."[8] Sa'eed now rejoiced in his decision and with renewed allegiance continued his pilgrimage.

When Kaka reached town the following day, a mob gathered around him threateningly. "We know why you let Sa'eed go. The Ferangis[9] sent you money." They were bent on wrecking his home. To placate them the Governor decided to destroy the house and banish Kaka, but the Imam Jum'eh intervened. He explained to the Governor: "Your Excellency knows very well that Sa'eed has been teaching me about Christianity. I personally

---

[7]Lu. 14:26
[8]Mk. 10:29-30
[9]Europeans

have sent him to Hamadan to learn more about the subject. Kaka is not to blame."

By this ruse Kaka was acquitted, but the people were unwilling to let Sa'eed slip from their grasp. So they drafted Shukrullah, an expert horseman, to hasten after him and bring him back, alive or dead. As he was about to mount his horse, a breathless messenger handed him an urgent summons from his chieftain. He was ordered to go at once to a distant village belonging to his overlord. So while he was speeding to this town eighty miles to the west, Sa'eed was proceeding to a city eighty miles to the southeast.

After five anxious days Sa'eed reached Hamadan in safety.

CHAPTER FOUR

In Hamadan

Ensconced in the security of the missionary home in
Hamadan and in free intercourse with Armenian and
Jewish Christians, Sa'eed kept repeating to himself the
words of Jami[1], *"Be bidarist ya Rabb ya be khab ast?"*
("O Lord, am I wide awake or am I dreaming?") Before
many days he assumed the costume of an Armenian and
let the hair grow on his shaved head, so as not to seem an
anomaly among his new friends. His white turban was
displaced by their black brimless, dome-shaped hat. "Mullah Sa'eed" became "Mirza Sa'eed," *mirza* being a term
of respect to denote a person of some education. He now
asked for baptism, but neither Mr. Hawkes nor the Armenians thought it wise, lest it stir up trouble with the
Moslem community. Meanwhile he was giving Mr.
Hawkes lessons in Persian and receiving instruction in
English and the Bible in return.

---
[1] A Persian poet of the 15th century.

Alas! this new freedom was short-lived. The Shah's brother, a fierce despot notorious for his ruthlessness, was appointed governor of Hamadan. The Armenians, viewing Sa'eed's open association with them as dangerous to themselves and a possible cause of persecution, were alarmed. With one accord they appealed to Mr. Hawkes to do something to forestall any untoward action. As a result, a barber was summoned, Sa'eed's head was shaved in Mohammedan style, and he was made to resume his former garb. He naturally followed the advice of these Christians, trusting that they knew what was best.

And now reaction set in. Some of the Armenians invited him to drink. In order to convince them that he had cast off all of his Islamic scruples[2] and anxious to imitate their ways, he readily participated in their "Christian" practices. Soon he was quaffing liquor freely. At the same time he mixed with Moslems, going to their public baths as one of them — a Christian with Christians and a Moslem with Moslems. Not even before his conversion had he been so cold spiritually. Invitations from Senneh to return to Islam and his old home were acknowledged with replies that were neither honest nor courageous. He even began to wonder if the Moslem belief that Christ was too glorious to suffer the shame and agony of the cross was not reasonable. He was wishing that the words of the Koran might be true: "They slew him not, and they crucified him not."[3] He was definitely slipping.

In the autumn of 1882 Dr. and Mrs. Alexander and Miss Annie Montgomery joined the missionary staff in Hamadan, soon to be followed by Miss Sherwood, who later became Mrs. Hawkes. Sa'eed was appointed their language teacher and he in turn studied English with Mrs. Alexander. Spring brought Dr. Alexander's medical supplies and he opened a clinic. Sa'eed, having made rapid progress in English, acted as his interpreter and helper.

---

[2]The use of intoxicants is specifically forbidden in the Koran.
[3]Sura 4:156

During these days Sa'eed chanced upon a hymn of that illustrious saint and missionary, Francis Xavier:

> *My God, I love thee; not because*
> *I hope for heaven thereby,*
> *Nor yet because who love thee not*
> *Must die eternally.*
>
> *Thou, O my Jesus, thou didst me*
> *Upon thy cross embrace;*
> *For me didst bear the nails and spear,*
> *And manifold disgrace;*
>
> *Yea, griefs and torments numberless,*
> *And sweat of agony,*
> *E'en death itself didst bear for one*
> *Who was thine enemy.*
>
> *Then why, O blessed Jesus Christ,*
> *Should I not love thee well?*
> *Not for the hope of winning heaven,*
> *Or of escaping hell;*
>
> *Not with the hope of gaining aught,*
> *Nor seeking a reward;*
> *But as thyself hast lovéd me,*
> *O ever-loving Lord!*

These words charmed him and kindled a glowing fire in his heart. They removed the scales from his eyes, so he said, and caused him to see himself and the cross of Christ in their true light. Mr. Hawkes' sermons at this time stirred him profoundly and Miss Montgomery greatly strengthened him by her unwavering friendship and her firm belief that God had a special mission for him. His spiritual aspirations flamed up anew.

Another thing that greatly encouraged Sa'eed was a visit by Kaka in the autumn of this year (1883). The two brothers embraced affectionately. Kaka showed no resentment; on the contrary, he appeared to have lost his old fanaticism and to accept Sa'eed's faith as established

Sa'eed and Kaka
as Young Men

fact. After many friendly discussions he returned home
with new impressions of Christianity. A restless year
elapsed. Again Kaka left Senneh on the pretext of visiting his brother, but while in Hamadan he sold the old
homestead. The Senneh ecclesiastics, however, declared it
the property of an apostate and so forfeit to the mosque.
Kaka refunded the money to the purchaser, thereby losing both house and furnishings. Though growing more
sympathetic toward Christianity, he found it hard to
believe that a man of his father's virtuous character could
have been misguided.

In these days a special season of prayer was held in
preparation for the quarterly communion. Sa'eed was

grieved that he was not allowed to participate in this sacrament because he had not been baptized — this Christian who longed for baptism, who had celebrated his first Lord's Supper in a vineyard, and who had suffered more for his faith than any of those who partook. During the service he devoted himself to prayer, especially for Kaka, and what was his inexpressible delight on returning home to find his brother studying the Bible and in the ensuing conversation ready to acknowledge the divinity of Christ. It was not long until Kaka made clear confession of his Christian faith.

Shortly after this Dr. Alexander took his wife to Teheran on account of her health. Sa'eed was asked to accompany them. While in the capital he came down with a serious attack of dysentery, so severe that it threatened to be fatal. As he meditated on his sickbed, he was troubled by the thought that on many occasions in talking with Moslems he had concealed his faith. He now vowed, if God spared him, never again to hide his light under a bushel.

He recovered and soon afterward he found ample opportunity to carry out his pledge, for he was sent to Kermanshah[4] on an evangelistic trip with Kasha Shimmon, an Assyrian pastor now serving in Hamadan. Here he found many Kurds from Senneh who had come there on business. It gave him especial joy to speak to them of his faith in Christ.

While in Kermanshah he met an Arab girl who had become a Roman Catholic. She had heard of him from friends. On meeting him she ventured a reproach: "Had you remained a Mohammedan, it would have been better than to become a Protestant,"

"But I am not a Protestant."

She smiled. "Then you are a Catholic?"

"O no, I am not!"

"What are you then?"

---

[4] Kermanshah is about 115 miles southwest of Hamadan on the road to. Baghdad.

"I find nothing in the Bible about Catholics or Protestants. I am a Christian." She had no answer.

In Dr. Alexander's clinic Sa'eed came in contact with scores of his fellow countrymen who came to Hamadan to trade or to find more competent medical treatment than was available in Senneh. As they sat in the waiting room, he read to them from the Bible or gave them Scriptures to take away. As he assisted in the clinic, he discovered what a powerful instrument medicine was for breaking down prejudice and generating confidence. Otherwise unapproachable, these men were willing in the clinic to discuss Christian teaching. So Sa'eed resolved to study medicine. Being in full agreement with this idea, Dr. Alexander became his enthusiastic teacher.

A new problem now arose. As private tutor in Persian to the children of Kasha Shimmon, Sa'eed enjoyed the welcome intimacy of his Christian home. After many months of teaching, during which his life had been imperceptibly woven into the colorful pattern of this worthy household, he found himself in love with one of the pastor's daughters — a love that was reciprocated. Rebka (Syriac for Rebecca) was a girl of noble character and exceptional intelligence, but her loveliness of face had been marred by a childhood attack of smallpox. He admired her keenness of mind and her sense of humor, but it was her spiritual nature which he prized above every feminine grace. She was a graduate of Fiske Seminary, the mission girls' high school in Urumia, and now a teacher in the mission school for girls in Hamadan. Not only would a marriage to such a girl satisfy the desires of his heart, but it would be an added proof to his Moslem acquaintances of the sincerity of his Christian profession.

When the romance was disclosed, trouble started. Rebka's impulsive father at once put his foot down. There was not only the difference in racial and religious backgrounds, but the union of one newly defected from Islam to a Christian girl would be a red flag flaunted before the

Moslem community and a source of jeopardy for both the couple and the Christians of the city. Appalled at the implications of such a marriage and jealous of the prestige of his family, the pastor ended the matter: "No! Absolutely not! It can never be!" And the girl's step-mother added her warning to that of her husband: "Who knows but some day he will turn back to Islam and bring reproach on you and disgrace on your daughter?"

When the Armenian community learned of the ro-mance, they were angry and frightened—angry at the couple and at Miss Montgomery, the sole sympathizer of the pair, for exposing them to danger, and frightened at the prospect of what the Moslems might do, if they learn-ed of the affair, especially since the pastor's home was in their quarter. Of course, they had reason for their alarm: it was unheard of that a Mohammedan (a mullah at that!) should apostatize and openly marry a Christian girl. They took their complaint to the missionaries and demanded Sa'eed's transfer elsewhere. When Kasha Shimmon re-proved Miss Montgomery for her encouragement of this ill-advised love affair, she replied: "Some day you will wish all your sons-in-law were like Sa'eed." On hearing this the Armenians were furious and insisted on his re-moval from Hamadan. Poor Sa'eed could not help feel-ing that Christians as well as Moslems were against him. Under the circumstances it seemed best to send him to Teheran.

The missionaries in Teheran were kind and sympa-thetic, but no sooner had Sa'eed arrived than he again fell severely ill. But if it was an occasion of physical distress, it was also a time of spiritual growth, for the unoccupied hours gave him ample leisure to develop the sense of God's presence. As he lay on his bed, he re-viewed his past life, examining it in detail. Had he committed any wrong that called for restitution? His sensitive conscience brought to mind a petty theft of long years back—some soap and tobacco worth about fifty cents. If Zaccheus was ready to restore fourfold any

unjust exaction,[5] he would restore eightfold. So he sent
the equivalent of four dollars to his old friend Faizullah,[6]
asking him to pay it to the right person with an explanation and a plea for pardon.

In the spring of 1887 Dr. Alexander returned from
furlough in America. Desirous of reopening his clinic,
he requested the return to Hamadan of his pupil assistant.
Sa'eed's joy on arrival was not shared by the Armenians,
who again anticipated trouble, especially since he soon
renewed his request for Rebka's hand. After repeated
appeals Kasha Shimmon agreed to the marriage on one
condition—Sa'eed's public baptism. If he thought by
this stipulation to intimidate the persistent lover, he was
greatly mistaken. On the contrary, Sa'eed was jubilant,
for he had repeatedly asked to be baptized, but his request
had always been denied for fear of Moslem reaction.

On the appointed day—April 10, 1887—in a full assembly room, with Mohammedans present, Sa'eed made his
confession of Christ and was solemnly baptized, thereby
becoming a pioneer in accepting this sacrament publicly
in a Moslem land. His joy knew no bounds. Rebka's
father now gave unreserved consent to the marriage, but
now another obstacle brought disappointment. Mr.
Hawkes declined to perform the ceremony on the ground
that Kasha Shimmon would never cease to blame him, if
Sa'eed were killed as a consequence.

Another year passed. Once again the beloved Kasha
Yohanan proved to be Sa'eed's good angel. While visiting
in Hamadan he agreed to perform the marriage rite. So
on June 4, 1888, a small company of friends gathered at
the bride's house to witness the simple ceremony.

While the service was in progress, Sa'eed's thoughts
went back twelve years to the time when he had prayed
in childish earnestness that if his father were to die, he

---

[5]Lu. 19:8
[6]After Sa'eed's departure from Senneh, Faizullah had risen to
leadership among the Naqshbandis, but from letters to Sa'eed it
was evident that he had found no peace of heart. Many years later
he died in an insane asylum in Teheran, a victim of alcoholism.

might be taken in the holy month of Ramazan. By the Mohammedan calendar this very day was the twelfth anniversary of his father's death. In his abstraction Sa'eed hesitated in answering the pastor's question as to his promised fidelity and love, whereupon Rebka nudged him in the ribs. "From then on," he used to say jokingly, "she has held the upper hand." Miss Montgomery opened her home to the bride and groom for their honeymoon.

Although all had been peaceful in the pastor's home as the family and guests shared in the happiness of the occasion, the choice of date had been most unfortunate, for the 21st of Ramazan is a day when Mohammedans in Iran are stirred to religious fervor in their commemoration of Ali's death. Moreover, the Armenians in fear and self-defense spread the news of the wedding about the community, carefully explaining that the bride was an Assyrian, not an Armenian, for Moslems in Iran often use the term "Armenian" of any Christian. As a result of all this, on the following day notices were posted in the bazaars and on the walls of mosques calling on the zealous faithful to avenge this unprecedented outrage of a Moslem renegade openly marrying a Christian. A large mob soon gathered. They closed their shops and began to march through the streets, calling with ominous shouts on their great *Imam:*[7] *"Ya Ali! Ya Ali!"* ("O Ali! O Ali!") — a signal for concerted action. They worked themselves up to a high pitch of frenzy, and some vowed never to rest until they had killed Sa'eed. Some prompt action had to be taken to disperse this angry rabble.

Providentially, the Governor and the Imam Jum'eh of Hamadan, two of the most influential dignitaries of the city, were both under obligation to Dr. Alexander for medical services. They both knew Sa'eed and liked him. Dr. Alexander lost no time in approaching them and urging them to quiet the storm.

---

[7]In Sunni Islam an imam is a leader of public prayers (See footnote 15 on page 27.) In Shiah Islam the imams were the successors of Mohammed in mediating his revelation. In Iran there are generally considered to have been twelve imams, of whom Ali was the first.

As soon as the raging mob reached the Governor's, he appeared on the balcony to speak. When some measure of quiet had been secured, he claimed to have received a letter from Sa'eed which put a totally different light on the whole situation. A hush fell over the crowd in the courtyard as he dramatically produced a letter from his pocket and pretended to read from it: "Whoever heard of a Moslem turning Christian? There is not a shred of truth in this rumor. It is a piece of sheer nonsense! . . ." Murmurs punctuated his deliberate reading until the letter was finished.

"It is my opinion," he went on to explain, "that similar assurances in Sa'eed's own hand have been sent to the Imam Jum'eh. There is no reason to doubt these statements." With these words he dismissed the people. He had proved himself a firm believer in Saadi's oft-quoted couplet:

Better a politic false invention
Than out-and-out truth that stirs up dissension.

The humorous sequel to this episode occurred when the Governor's impertinent nephew, confident of Sa'eed's integrity, offered his uncle fifty tomans[8] for a letter in Sa'eed's handwriting such as he had read. The challenge was not accepted! It was the nephew himself who afterward related this incident to Sa'eed.

The Imam Jum'eh, on his part, was similarly engaged at the Central Mosque, where another crowd had assembled to hear a verdict pronounced on the apostate. In this way the mobs were quieted and dispersed.

Meanwhile the Armenians were trembling in their homes behind barred doors. Kasha Shimmon sat peacefully at his gate smoking his pipe. Sa'eed also was calm. Psalm 91, which he had read on the day of his marriage, had given him assurance. He called it "the Lord's wedding present."

But for his bride the following months proved a time of

8A toman in those days was worth in the neighborhood of a dollar.

great anxiety. In every flickering shadow in the courtyard she saw a creeping figure. Every noise in the night
made her jump out of her sleep with palpitating heart.
Many an evening, on returning from the clinic, Sa'eed
found her waiting behind the locked door, distraught by
a host of imagined possibilities. She was especially
worried if on his calls in Moslem homes he was offered
food or a glass of tea, but he would console her with
Christ's promise to his disciples, "If they drink any deadly
thing, it shall not hurt them."[9] She wasn't so sure!

---

[9]Mk. 16:18

CHAPTER FIVE

Journeys in Iran and Abroad

In the meantime Sa'eed worked indefatigably at his medical studies. Along with modern texts he pored over Razi[1] and Avicenna,[2] often till after midnight. As he became more experienced he was entrusted with greater responsibility. Along with his work in Dr. Alexander's clinic he was testifying to his faith before all classes of people. From his headquarters in Hamadan his activities extended to neighboring villages by numerous itinerating trips. Medicine and evangelism went hand in hand: this was his life purpose.

In mid-December 1889 Sa'eed made one of these trips to Sultanabad (now Arak), a city to the southeast of

---

[1]Razi (or Rhazes) was a famous Persian physician who flourished in the early part of the 10th century, practising in Rai (or Rhages), whose ruins are near Teheran, and in Baghdad. His medical writings were widely studied in the Middle Ages in Latin translation.

[2]Avicenna was an even more celebrated Persian physician born near the close of the same century. See Chapter 11.

Hamadan. He was accompanied by a Jewish convert and a servant. While here he called twice on the Imam Jum'eh of the city. The second time he found him attended by a group of his pupils and followers. The Imam Jum'eh took exception to the Bible: "There are statements in the Old Testament contrary to our concept of God."

"What, for instance?" asked Sa'eed.

"Your Bible represents God as lacking omniscience. It depicts him as saying, 'Adam, where art thou?' "[3]

"If you reject the Bible for that, then you must discard the Koran also, for in it God says, 'What is that in thy right hand, Moses?' "[4]

In confusion the Imam Jum'eh quickly changed the subject.

Some days later he sent Sa'eed eight pages of writing in defense of Islam, inviting him to reply, which he did. Then came twenty pages, in the course of which he called Sa'eed an enemy of Islam who had deserted the true religion because he found it too exacting!

At this point came a letter from Dr. Alexander requesting Sa'eed's return to Hamadan. Some days after he got back he received a letter from a friend in Sultanabad, who wrote: "It was a good thing you were not here. The Imam Jum'eh and fifteen mullahs went to your house to kill you."

During the Noruz holidays[5] Sa'eed went with Mr. Hawkes to call on a general of the army. Conversation quite naturally turned to religion. The general resented something Sa'eed said and after they left he vowed to put a bullet through "that impudent Kurd." Through a mullah whom he had primed he sent a complaint to the governor. The next day a servant came from that

---

[3]Gen. 3:9
[4]Sura 20:18
[5]Noruz (meaning "New Day") is the first day of spring and the first day of the Iranian new year. Celebrations last for thirteen days. It is a time for calling on officials and friends.

official with a curt summons that presaged trouble. Upon being ushered into the Governor's presence, in accordance with Iranian courtesy Sa'eed took a seat near the door, but his host asked him to come nearer and inquired, so that all others present could hear, "How do you treat dysentery?" Then, asking Sa'eed to come still closer, he whispered: "Last night a mullah came to me accusing you of speaking incessantly against Islam. I calmed him down, telling him you were a medical student and explaining that medical students as a rule have no religion. So go now, and don't give the mullahs occasion for further complaint." That was all. Sa'eed left, greatly relieved. Later, the general who was responsible for this incident became one of Sa'eed's friends.

Upon the termination of his contract with the Mission in 1891 Sa'eed decided to make a trip to Urumia, whither Rebka had already gone with their little daughter Sarah[6] to visit her relatives. This adventure gave him an opportunity to give a Christian message in his native tongue in some of the border towns in Kurdistan and further on to visit his dear friend, Kasha Yohanan. The pastor introduced him with great pride and joy to the people of his parish, whom he delighted by preaching to them in Syriac.

In Urumia he met with a group of Moslem converts who had suffered much persecution from their neighbors. He reminded them that from the first, Christians had had to endure tribulation: "The blood of the martyrs has always been the seed of the Church. In no country has Christianity been established without some sacrifice of life. So let us be prepared. Who knows for which of us the lot will first fall?" Little did Sa'eed realize that his prophetic words would soon be fulfilled, for just about two years later one of that very group, Mirza Ibrahim, drank the cup of martyrdom. That faithful soldier of the cross could not withold his testimony even in his dungeon, where he died from injuries inflicted by the criminals to whom he was chained.

---

[6]Born November 1890.

On his return to Hamadan Sa'eed was asked to renew his contract with the Mission. He was reluctant to do so, but the clinic was closed because Dr. Alexander had terminated his missionary service and patients were in desperate need. So he agreed to work for another year till a new physician should arrive from America. He was now in full charge of the dispensary—doctor, druggist, and often nurse, all in one. These burdensome duties, combined with strenuous study at night, both medical and religious, were a danger to his health. Added to all this came an epidemic of cholera. Taking his family outside of the town for safety, he himself labored faithfully in the city among the sick and dying till he was near a breakdown.

In the late fall of that year (1892) the Moslems of Hamadan threatened to massacre their Jewish neighbors. Sa'eed was now living in the Jewish quarter of the city to be near the dispensary and Rebka was teaching in a mission school for Hebrew children. This locality now became a dangerous spot for the family, to which had been added a son, Samuel, born in early November. For their safety the Mission moved them to the dispensary compound and to make the move doubly safe, it was carried out at night under cover of darkness. The massacre did not materialize.

In the following April Dr. Holmes arrived from America to take up Dr. Alexander's work. Sa'eed's period of contract having ended, he wished to terminate his service with the Mission and so tendered his resignation. He had served faithfully for twelve years as language teacher, doctor's assistant, and then physician. During this time he had received great benefit from the missionaries: they had befriended him; they had taught him English and medicine; they had helped him spiritually. This debt he felt had been sufficiently repaid by his long period of service, so that he was now at liberty to break away.

To one of his independent spirit it was galling to be at the beck and call of others. To be subjected to the

taunt that he was professing Christianity for pay, especially when his salary was so meager, was unbearable. He
yearned to be free, to work out his own salvation, to be
subject to no dictate save the will of God as he understood it. So he determined to fare forth on his own. This
resolve—not an easy one to make—he regarded ever
after in retrospect as an important turning point in his
life. He used to say: "This decision is as precious to me
as that taken with God's help on the day I refused to
return to Senneh with Kaka. For both these crucial
decisions in my life I render daily thanks to God."

Four reasons now impelled him to take a trip abroad.
In the first place, the best way to launch out on his new
career was to get away for a time from his former associ-
ates and environment. Secondly, he felt the need of a
change of climate and a rest from the grind of heavy
routine. The pressure of work had worn him down to
a state of neurasthenia, attended by insomnia and indigestion. In addition to these reasons, he felt the need
of further medical training. What he could learn from a
single physician and from books with no laboratory save
his own practice was altogether too limited. He wanted
to go to England or America, where he could study under
experienced professors. A fourth factor in his decision
was the fulfilment of a dream very dear to his heart—
the attainment of spiritual perfection. He had met in
Hamadan a Swedish missionary, Hogberg by name, who
claimed to have achieved such an ideal. If such an ac-
complishment were possible, he would leave no stone
unturned to bring it about. Mr. Hogberg had invited
him to Sweden, where he hoped to realize this ambition.

Impelled by this inner urge, he set out for Sweden,
traveling as cheaply as possible with the help of borrowed
funds, later repaid in full. He reached Stockholm June
9, 1893. At the headquarters of the Swedish Mission he
was told that they intended to support him while he was
pursuing his studies in England, so that on their completion he would join them in their labors in Turkestan

or China. He was aghast and protested that his heart was in Persia and that he had no thought of going elsewhere.

After a few days Mr. Hogberg telephoned him from Oxholm, asking Sa'eed to join him there, bringing along his Kurdish clothes and dagger. Then followed a long trip around Sweden with Mr. Hogberg, traveling by train or boat or on foot, speaking in town after town. His Kurdish costume was a great attraction—striped silk turban, knee-length tunic held together by a massive twisted sash, open long-sleeved jacket, baggy trousers, slipper-like shoes, and to top it all, a short, curved, ivory-handled dagger at his waist. His manner was dignified. His accounts of Kurdistan and of life and work in Persia fascinated his hearers and elicited high praise.

But withal, the experience was utterly dissatisfying. He was not getting the rest he needed. On the contrary, strange faces day after day, new audiences, the strain of speaking so frequently in public, and the fatigue of constant travel taxed his strength and brought nervous excitement. The indigestion and sleeplessness of Hamadan now reappeared in alarming fashion.

Nor was there any indication of his attaining his other objectives. He was receiving support from others. He was getting no opportunity for medical study. And as for spiritual perfection, he was not even making progress in that direction. When he sought to speak on a spiritual theme, Hogberg demanded "interesting things about the customs of the Kurds and the beliefs of the Mohammedans." All the applause and compliments he received served only to engender self-conceit. His conservative convictions grated upon the liberals he met. It seemed to him that those to whom he looked for perfection had strayed far from the truth. The diversity of belief among different denominations — Lutherans, Roman Catholics, Free Church, Greek Orthodox, Free Thinkers — shook him deeply. Upsetting thoughts would come to him: "Don't you see there is nothing in Christianity after all?

There has been no need of all these severe trials you have endured these many years. Do you think you, a simple Kurd, know better than all these highly educated men?"

Sa'eed finally became so exhausted from all these experiences that a doctor prescribed hydropathic treatment. However, his weakness only increased and he was ordered to bed. Even here he grew weaker. Sleeplessness became more marked. The slightest movement, even the exertion of thinking deeply, brought on palpitation of the heart. Over and again he wished he might die.

After many days a change came. He could sleep a few hours each night. Short walks in the woods soothed his nerves and helped restore his strength. When he had grown somewhat stronger, he was kneeling at his bedside one morning, praying for that perfection that seemed so elusive. Of a sudden there flashed into his mind with a radiance of light the words of the apostle John: "We know that, when he shall appear, we shall be like him; for we shall see him as he is."[7] Twenty simple words, only one as long as two syllables, but how luminous! "When he appears" — *then*, not now. "If it is *then*," he thought, "that we shall be like Christ, how foolish to expect it now!" A great wave of relief swept over him. The anxiety for speedy attainment of perfection left him. The grace of God had triumphed over his inner conflict.

Returning to Stockholm, Sa'eed was advised by a doctor to take a long rest by the sea. He found a place not far away where kind friends watched over him. Most of his time was spent in bed. Occasionally he took short walks. All went well until one night, due to a sudden drop in temperature, he had a severe chill which developed into influenza and bronchitis. Weakness and depression reduced him to the depths of despair. Doubts again assailed him, but they were dispelled by returning strength and the memory of God's goodness to him over the years—his guidance to faith in Christ, his deliverance

---

[7] I Jo. 3:2

in times of danger, his illumining light when ways were dark.

The first month of autumn was nearly over when Sa'eed decided to leave for England. In this decision he was helped by the advice of Swedish doctors, who recommended that he study in London. Sweden had been a disappointment. Would England be any better? He wondered.

The North Sea crossing had an important effect on Sa'eed's future. The weather was stormy and the sea rough. Since he was acting as "ship's doctor," an Irish couple, Mr. and Mrs. Cavanaugh, called upon him for relief from their seasickness. They became so interested in his story that they agreed to introduce him to a doctor friend of theirs in London, a Dr. Charles Warren, who would both help him spiritually and advise him in his medical studies.

Sa'eed's first impressions of England were anything but favorable. His first lodging place in London was the Scandinavian Sailors' Temperance Home, to which a letter of introduction gave him entry. It was near a railroad station and looked out on a maze of tracks and signals. The neighborhood was crowded with row upon row of dingy buildings soiled with the grime of many years. Myriads of crooked chimneys and windows with broken panes completed a picture of sordid poverty.

However, as his walks took him farther afield, he glimpsed the wonders of civilization on an even larger scale than he had seen in Sweden—telephones, streetcars, wide avenues lighted by gas or electricity, policemen at crossroads, spacious hospitals, universities, museums, libraries, homes for the aged and infirm — all astonishing to a stranger from Persia. Yet what were these to quench his spiritual thirst? It was not long before his heart was sick of the great metropolis.

His efforts to get in touch with church activities were frustrating. He first went to a series of evangelistic meetings in the vicinity of his lodgings, but the methods used to urge inquirers to make professions of faith seemed crude and superficial: they reminded him of his initiation into the Naqshbandis of Senneh. He received two letters from a gentleman he had met on the boat, encouraging him to seek out a Methodist clergyman, who would assuredly help him. Twice he called by appointment, waited an hour for the minister to appear, then left disheartened. An invitation to call came from the secretary of a missionary society, but even here he failed to meet with the sympathetic consideration that he needed. One night he visited St. Paul's cathedral: the liturgical worship reminded him of the Catholic services he had seen in Senneh and had no meaning for him. He went to church after church and meeting after meeting all over the city, unsuccessful in finding the spiritual uplift that he sought.

The Cavanaughs, however, lived up to their promise and introduced Sa'eed to Dr. and Mrs. Warren, who were earnest Christians and extremely friendly. Dr. Warren was a capable physician and proved of great help in guiding him in the choice of courses of study and the most suitable schools for his work. Not only that, but the Warrens took him into their home as one of the family. He lived with them for nearly two years and they became lifelong friends.

They introduced him to many people, a goodly number of whom, like themselves, were Plymouth Brethren.[8] He was invited to their meetings and was greatly pleased with their very first session. "I see you have no minister," he observed after this introductory visit. "Is it because all Christians are priests?"[9] He had quickly sensed one of their distinctive tenets. He found the group composed of a goodly number of well-educated people, such as doctors, writers, and mathematicians, side by side with simple, ordinary folk. Often the least suspected

---

[8]The Plymouth Brethren or "Brethren" (as they call themselves) are a religious group that meet without formal organization. The movement originated in Plymouth, England, whence the name.

[9]Rev. 1:6

person manifested a remarkable knowledge of the Bible. But though he was in accord with much that he heard and saw, he was determined after his disillusionment in Sweden not to rush into the arms of any group. For fifteen months he attended their meetings before he decided, after careful search, deep thought, and earnest prayer, to be associated with them.

For him the Brethren represented a group whose views were preeminently suited to his own temper and convictions. The Bible, which had been his mainstay ever since his conversion, constituted the sole authority on which their beliefs and worship were based. They recognized no teacher other than the Holy Spirit. The limitation of the ministry to one individual, therefore, seemed to infringe on the office of the Spirit in the distribution of gifts to the various members of the assembly. The person of Christ provided the center around which their hearts were united in adoration and praise. Their worship was the simplest. The fellowship was warm and intimate. Sa'eed's association with this group brought him deep and increasing satisfaction and the fulfilment of a long-cherished dream of Christian aspiration. He had found a spiritual home and the realization of an abiding peace.

During this time Sa'eed was pursuing his medical studies. He felt special need of training in anatomy and physiology, for his pursuit of these two subjects in Persia had been chiefly book study without laboratory work. Dissection of human bodies was regarded as contrary to the law of Islam and hence at that time was not permitted in Persia.[10] So he attended courses in these two branches of medicine at Cook's School of Anatomy and Physiology in London. He also devoted some time to the study of pharmacology and bacteriology.

One day in Dr. Cook's school he was dissecting the abdominal region of a human body. When Dr. Cook saw

---

[10]During the reign of Reza Shah (1925-41) a medical school was opened in Teheran, where modern methods were introduced.

his finished work, he complimented Sa'eed on its neatness and the excellent demonstration of the parts exposed.

"That is excellent," he said. "Very nice, indeed."

"Thank you, sir."

Dr. Cook examined Sa'eed's work further, constantly mumbling his satisfaction. "How much have you paid the attendant toward the dissection of this body?"

"Five guineas, sir."

"Um . . . then you owe five more."

"Yes, sir."

"You do beautiful work. Keep the five guineas you owe. In return I want you to do special dissections for me for class demonstration." Sa'eed gladly accepted the offer, for he was in need of money.

In the evening Dr. Cook came again to examine Sa'eed's further work. "Well done! That is excellent," he said with genuine admiration.

Pointing to the adrenal glands, which he had skillfully exposed, Sa'eed asked: "Of what use are these two small glands on the kidneys? What is their function?"

"Nothing very important," replied the teacher.

"I have read somewhere," Sa'eed ventured, "that their tuberculosis gives rise to Addison's disease."

"So they used to say, but in reality they are not important and have no distinctive function."

"But look here, sir; each one of these glands is fed by three relatively large arteries. Such attention from the wise Creator for no use seems improbable."

After a moment's reflection Dr. Cook said, "In your country you must be quite an authority."

"You are making fun of me," answered Sa'eed.

"Not at all; I am serious. Until now no one has raised the point you are making. I am sure you are right."

The next day he presented Sa'eed with an autographed copy of his own publications as a souvenir of this conversation. Not long afterward Sa'eed read about the sensational discovery of the physiological effect of adrenalin by Oliver and Shaefer. And only now are scientists beginning to understand something of the very important role that several other hormones of this gland play in the normal functioning of the body.

Another study to which Sa'eed devoted much time was ophthalmology. During his years of practice in Persia he had been struck with the appalling amount of damaged eyesight and actual blindness due to neglect of the eyes and lack of timely treatment. Accordingly, he took a course in this branch of medicine at the General Hospital in Croydon and later on another course at the Central Hospital.

At the latter institution his instructor complimented him: "Fortunate are the patients you will treat." Astonished, Sa'eed asked the reason for this word of commendation. "Because," replied the doctor, "your minute care in diagnosis is excellent."

In the spring of 1895 Dr. Patrick Manson, who later became the founder and director of the famous London School of Tropical Medicine and was knighted for his distinguished services, offered a special course at St. George's Hospital for instruction in this specialty which was his particular interest. As yet there had been no such course available in London. Sa'eed was the third student to enroll in this class. The instruction in these tropical diseases was given with the aid of adequate specimens and demonstrations, all of which proved of immense value to Sa'eed later on in his practice in Iran.

Here, as in all the institutions he attended, Sa'eed won the respect of his teacher, who treated him as a friend and colleague rather than as a mere student. On completion of his studies, when Sa'eed went to take his leave, Sir Patrick requested him to send back some blood slides from his homeland. Several years later, when Sa'eed was traveling in the south of Persia as a private physician to Prince Ain-ud-Dowleh, a unique opportunity presented itself for granting this request, since the Prince had a retinue of 5,000 people who represented a good cross section of various elements of the country. Sa'eed prepared many boxes of blood smears and sent them to London. Sir Patrick acknowledged their safe arrival, adding, "I shall see what I can find in the blood of the descendants of Cyrus and Darius."

And so came to a close two years of life in London that began inauspiciously, but finished full of promise. Although delicate health had at times necessitated a break in his work, Sa'eed was sustained with the joyful anticipation of a more effective service to his own people.

A farewell tea was given him by his group of Brethren, at the close of which prayers were offered that God would keep him amid the difficulties and dangers he might have to face in the homeland. At the conclusion Sa'eed rose and said: "When I look back at the way the Lord has led me, I say, 'What hath God wrought!' I cannot express how much I owe him. He has satisfied my longing soul. In your prayers tonight you have been expressing so very much my own feelings. A good deal has been said about the trials and opposition I may meet, but I am not afraid of them, for I have learned that trouble is sweet. Rather, I am afraid of myself, of self-confidence and self-reliance. Pray for me about this. I commend you to God. There will be difficulties, but he will help us. May we go on, thinking only of him and not of ourselves."

Dr. Warren accompanied him to Cardiff, whence he was to sail for Batoum on the Black Sea. His parting gift was a beautiful doctor's bag supplied with all sorts of medicinal necessities, which Sa'eed found indispensable in his future work. Other friends furnished him with surgical equipment with which to continue his practice in Persia.

He reached Hamadan October 30, 1895. He had been away from home two and a half years.

CHAPTER SIX

Practising Under Difficulties

On return to Persia, Sa'eed found disorder and turmoil on every hand. The extravagances of Naser-ed-Din Shah, his acquisition of ruinous foreign loans, and the ever-multiplying concessions made by him to foreigners had given rise to wide discontent. There was threat of an imminent popular uprising. Growing disaffection between the Shah and the clergy bred disrespect for law and authority. Because of the power of the ecclesiastics, many unprincipled individuals had donned the mullah's turban and set themselves up as administrators of justice. The lives and property of the common people were easy spoil for anyone who could exercise sufficient force. They were uncertain days for anybody. How much more so for an apostate from Islam!

Within a short while Sa'eed and his family moved into a home of their own. The doctor's English friends

had not only helped them with his needs while he was
in London but had sent substantial sums for the support
of the family. By careful management Rebka had saved
up enough of this so that by borrowing a small balance
she had bought the new house.

Sa'eed soon was informed that he would have to
pay a certain assessment for the *sayyids* (descendants of
Mohammed). He consulted a friendly mullah, who
agreed: "It is a rule of Islam that *zimmis* (a disparaging
term to denote non-Moslems under Mohammedan rule)
have to pay this tax."

Sa'eed replied: "I willingly accept the humiliation of
being called a *zimmi*, for I owe much to Christianity."

The mullah sighed. "All who have come to know you
see that."

Afterward the same man had often to apply to Sa'eed
for treatment for trachoma. When finally healed, he
sent the doctor a costly diamond ring, which he courteously refused. The success of the cure was more to Sa'eed
than the jewel. Early in his career he made it a rule
never to accept fees from the clergy. He often followed
the same custom with his fellow Kurds.

Medical practice filled the doctor's time to the full.
"Office hours" had no meaning in those days. People
expected to see the physician whenever it suited them to
call. And sometimes, when a doctor asked a patient what
was troubling him, he might get the answer, "You're
the doctor; you ought to know, not I." And since he had
to be his own druggist and nurse, Sa'eed's work was most
demanding.

His practice was sufficient to enable the family to live
in reasonable comfort. Payments for medical services
were in large part in kind—carpets, sheep, grain, butter,
sugar cones, etc. Some of these Rebka exchanged or sold
to get cash. The friends in England helped with other
needs of the home. Among these gifts was a cast-iron cook
stove—the wonder and envy of friends and neighbors.
Another present was a Singer hand sewing machine: for

weeks there were lady callers to exclaim in astonishment over this marvel. For the children there were blocks, toys, dolls, balloons, and paint boxes.

Meanwhile the political situation continued to deteriorate. In May 1896 Naser-ed-Din Shah was assassinated. He was succeeded by his son, Mozaffar-ed-Din, in whose timid reign the authority of the throne suffered further decline. Fresh disturbances broke out. Travel was unsafe. Religious and political factions fought each other. Old feuds were revived. Rising discontent with the new king tended to guide the whole current of events toward the inevitable culmination — a revolution, out of which was born a constitutional form of government.

During these precarious days Sa'eed had numerous Kurds as patients. One afternoon some Kurds from his father's native district near the Turkish border came to the clinic. One of them, with his dagger in his sashbelt, looked especially wild, restless like a tiger ready to spring on his prey. Fortunately, after receiving the needed medicines, they left quietly, but on the following day the doctor received a letter from a Catholic friend who was staying at the same carvanserai as the Kurds, warning him against them. Such warnings were not without basis, for a party of his fellow countrymen actually had been hatching a plot to kill him. In fact, one day a wild Kurd attacked Kaka on the street with his dagger, mistaking him for his brother. Providentially, Kaka was able to defend himself till others came to his aid.

Mozaffar-ed-Din Shah had no particular concern for Christians, who had enjoyed some degree of liberty under his father. There was now practically no religious freedom in the country, not so much through active interference as through his indifference, which allowed the clergy to usurp more power. What they ordered in matters of civil or religious jurisdiction no one could gainsay. It was becoming increasingly dangerous to bear witness to his Christian faith, yet Dr. Sa'eed was talking with his patients, and on each Thursday and Sunday afternoon he held Bible readings in his house. Those who attended were mostly Armenians and Jewish converts, but there were also Moslems who had had private discussion with him and sought more light.

It was at this time that a prominent ecclesiastic in Hamadan sent for Sa'eed to attend his father, also a mullah, well known for his piety and learning. The doctor found the sick man in the last stages of cancer. Medically, the case was hopeless. Possibly he could help him spiritually. So, while the patient was looking anxiously for the verdict, in the presence of all who were there Sa'eed asked: "After so many years of service to God are you not glad to go to meet him?" With an expression of intense fear the mullah turned away his head without answering.

"Well, my dear sir," Sa'eed continued, "I can do nothing for you," and left. The next day the mullah died.

The most learned ecclesiastic in Hamadan, having heard of Sa'eed's question of the dying man, sent for him. When he called, he found the cleric smoking his water pipe. "Well," said the mullah smiling, "so you asked the old man if he wasn't ready to meet God? Wonderful! Aren't you afraid to meet him yourself?"

"Not in the least," replied Sa'eed, and then went on to explain why, as a Christian, he could face death with complete assurance. This was amazing doctrine for the three Moslems present and resulted in a long and friendly conversation, during which the mullah opened his Koran at random for augury.[1] Thereupon he asked Sa'eed, "Do you do the same with the Bible?" This gave an opportunity to explain that Christians take their problems to God in prayer and trust him to give needed guidance in

[1]The "cutting of the Koran," known as *istikhareh*, is a very common practice among Moslems. The book is opened at random and the first verse on which the eye lights is supposed to give divine guidance on the matter in hand. Missionary surgeons are sometimes obliged to delay an urgently needed operation because of an unfavorable augury.

such a way as he deems best. The Moslems still thought their way more effective.

Toward the end of that summer (1896) Hamadan was thrown into a panic by an embroilment between two parties of mullahs, the *Akhunds* and the *Sheikhis*. The major cause of the strife arose from the fact that the Sheikhis extolled the twelve Imams[2] in terms of extreme adulation. The Akhunds thought such glorification was blasphemous, and they looted the houses of the Sheikhis, some of whom were killed, while others fled. On one poor fellow they poured kerosene and burned him alive in the street. No one ventured out after dark. A cavalry regiment, consisting chiefly of Kurdish outlaws, and a regular infantry battalion were sent to Hamadan to maintain order.

In the midst of this turmoil Rebka gave birth to her third child, Lemuel (August 1896). At night it was difficult to keep the children quiet, for they could hear the whizzing of bullets overhead as they lay in their beds on the flat roof, their sleeping quarters in hot weather.

During this time of riot Sa'eed sought out the persecuted Sheikhis in places where merciful friends sheltered them. Daily he treated many sick and wounded. This roused the anger of the Akhunds. More than once, going about town, he heard it said: "The Sheikhis are killed and scattered. Why is this infidel permitted to live?"

The leading mullah who was the chief cause of the tumult sent for Sa'eed one day and sought to justify himself: "These Sheikhis say blasphemous things about our Imams. If the Jews were to say such things about Christ, what would you do?"

"As a Christian I would treat them kindly. Christ prayed for his enemies when they crucified him. He bids us do the same." The mullah looked down with no answer. He was later sent to Teheran under heavy escort on the Shah's order and the disturbance subsided.

---

[2]See footnote page 63.

Among the Kurdish patients who came to Dr. Sa'eed was a merchant from Saujbulagh (now Mihabad), Mirza Hosein by name, a zealous Moslem. He started religious discussion and when he found his arguments answered, he became abusive. Sa'eed expected never to see him again, but the next day he showed up, saying, "Please do something to hurt me, so that I can become angry with you." The doctor opened his Bible and read: "If thine enemy hunger, feed him; if he thirst, give him drink . . . Be not overcome of evil, but overcome evil with good."[3] "How can I hurt you when I believe in such words as these?"

With oaths Mirza Hosein replied that all this meekness was the fruit of deceit. "By my father's soul, you are wrong. You have been misled. In vain you suffer so much. Go on, get drunk. Do anything you like. Enjoy the world while you can, for I swear by God your place is hell." Then he added, "If anyone had talked to me like that, I would have killed him." When he left, Sa'eed honored him by accompanying him to the door and adjusting his shoes for him.[4] Mirza Hosein told some friends that while he had used unbearable words to Sa'eed, he had received only honor in return.

A few days later he came back. While receiving treatment, he evidenced his disquiet of soul: "Had God made me fall off my horse and break my neck, I should have been a happier man. I am unspeakably sorry for my visit to Hamadan at this time. May God grant me to die a Moslem!"

The doctor removed his shoes and socks, showed him the two scars on his legs, and told him the story of his own anguish of soul in search of peace. He concluded: "I trust the same gracious God, who in spite of these scars

---

[3]Rom. 12:20-21

[4]When a guest entered a house, he would slip off his shoes and leave them, toes toward the door. When he left, it would be a mark of courtesy for the host to turn the shoes around, so they would be in the right position for the departing guest to put on. This office was usually performed by a servant or by an inferior for a superior.

gave me no peace until he had led me to know him, will do the same for you."

A friend of Mirza Hosein from whose neck Sa'eed had removed a tumor wished to return to Saujbulagh. Before he left, the doctor desired to take him to see Dr. Holmes, who at that time was spending the summer out in the country. Mirza Hosein accompanied them. When the trio were well out of town, Mirza Hosein asked, "How do you, an apostate, dare to ride outside the city with us?" To his friend he added, "When Allah's time for waging war comes, one Moslem will kill ten unbelievers."

"In my case," said Sa'eed, "there is no need to wait for an appointed time. It is always lawful and even meritorious to kill an apostate."

"Had I run across you before I came to know you, or even the first time I came to see you, I might have done it, but now . . . how can I blind my eyes with my own hands?" He kept on talking all the way. Finally, in desperation: "I plead with you to say just once, 'Mohammed is the apostle of God!' " These few words would have saved Sa'eed from any threat of death, but of course he refused.

It was dark as they journeyed back. Despite Rebka's fears for her husband he returned home safely.

Some days later Mirza Hosein came to say good-bye. Sa'eed expressed the hope of some day seeing him in Saujbulagh, but he replied, "Don't ever come to Kurdistan or you will surely be killed." Then he added: "Before taking my leave I have brought you a small present. Though it is unworthy, I hope you will make me happy by accepting it." The gift was a fine saddle, for he knew the doctor was using a borrowed one on the horse he had recently purchased to lessen the fatigue of his daily rounds.

"I'm sure my horse and I appreciate your kindness," was the smiling reply .

Mirza Hosein grasped Sa'eed's hand firmly in both of

his. "May the Lord protect you, honored doctor." He sighed and was gone.

At the turn of the century Dr. Sa'eed was called by Prince Ain-ud-Dowleh, son-in-law of the Shah and Governor General of several provinces in the southwest of Persia, to attend his wife. For a whole year following he served as private physican to the Prince and his retinue of 5,000 people on an inspection trip through the territory of his assignment. During this time he was instrumental in healing a gunshot wound in the Prince's leg that had resulted in a gangrenous condition and threatened amputation. Following this he had occasion to serve the royal household, which he did with such satisfaction that the Shah wished to retain him as Court Physician, but Sa'eed had no desire to spend his talents on a select few. He felt that his life and abilities should be at the service of all who wished his help, privileged and underprivileged alike.

Before his return to Hamadan the Shah, in appreciation of his skillful service, awarded him the title of *Mo'atamed-us-Sultan* (The One Trusted by the King) and an annual stipend for life of 200 tomans. Sa'eed refused to use the title and many of his friends never knew that he had it, although other physicians who had secured titles, usually by purchase, were for the most part eager to be known by them. As for the emolument, it was paid only irregularly and finally discontinued along with other royal pensions early in the reign of Reza Shah with the payment of a small lump sum which Sa'eed humorously characterized as "the extreme unction of the Persian government."

In January 1901 Dr. Sa'eed decided to make a second trip to Urumia. Biting winter winds and such blinding sand and snow that the doctor on his Arab horse and the servant behind on a mule had trouble at times in finding the road made the journey not only difficult but again and again hazardous. For miles at a stretch through desolate country their guides were the telegraph poles or the whistle of the wind across the wires. One day the snowdrifts were so bad that they dragged only a painful six miles. The boiled water in the doctor's flask was solid ice. The tea houses along the road were few and far between, but when reached, their stuffy warmth brought comfort, and the little glasses of tea, hot from the samovar, were refreshing.

One day, after losing their way and finally finding it again, they were welcomed into a village home. As soon as they were seated under the *kursi*, the host boasted that he was a *sayyid*. "And I am a Christian," the doctor announced. The descendant of Mohammed was horrified, refused to eat with him, and early in the morning hurried him off, saying that the Christian had brought shame on his house. But it was no shame to purloin the doctor's jackknife!

On another day of hail and sleet the couple arrived at dark at a further village where they coaxed a young man to give them a night's lodging. The family soon found they had admitted a Christian. The mother began beating her breast because of the disgrace. When she saw Sa'eed's wet coat hanging on the wall, she reproached her son: "Why did you bring this man in?   Now I shall have to scrape off the whitewash!" Then she added: "However, let the guest say, 'There is no god but God and Mohammed is the apostle of God,' and he will become clean." To think that the doctor would sell his faith for a night's lodging! On leaving in the morning he paid four times the usual amount for his brief entertainment, but they claimed it wasn't enough to purify what he had defiled.

The last stage to Zenjan, one of two main cities on his route, was the worst yet. Sa'eed's moustache was frozen to the borders of his hood. Frost covered his lashes and eyebrows. In a filthy hovel of a room in the first caravanserai he came to he went to bed, piling on him everything he had, but he was too cold to sleep. Fortunately, the next day an Armenian friend transferred him to his own home, where he stayed several days to rest. Here

he was able to give much Christian instruction to several
Armenians and to show a Jewish Babi[4] inconsistencies in
his sacred book, the *Bayan.*

On the road from Zenjan to Tabriz, the second city of
size in Iran, is a difficult mountain pass called Qaflankuh,
which in those days had to be crossed.[5] As Sa'eed was
traversing this pass in the early morning light, his horse
suddenly slowed its pace and neighed in alarm. Sa'eed
looked up and saw four wolves ahead. Turning his horse
around like a flash, he galloped off to a distance, then
stopped to look back. It occurred to him to give the
Kurdish cries believed to frighten away wild beasts.
The trick worked: the wolves trotted off. Just then the
sun's rays burst over the eastern hills, bringing to Sa'eed's
mind the words of the Psalmist: "Thou makest darkness
wherein all the beasts of the forest do creep forth. . . The
sun ariseth, they gather themselves together, and lay
them down in their dens."[6]

After many more halts and varied experiences, including a severe attack of bronchitis in Tabriz which all but
developed into pneumonia, the pair finally arrived at
Urumia, eighty-nine days after leaving home. All along
the way, in town, in village, and in caravanserai, Sa'eed
had preached Christ, and though often exhausted, had
gladly responded to the call of the sick. When he reached
the Urumia plain, now under a thick mantle of snow, and
once again passed through the neat villages and hamlets
of its Christian community, his heart filled with joy.
Ever since his first visit ten years before he had been
captivated by the beauty of the district, and the warm-
hearted reception accorded him by the Assyrians as to
an adopted son.

Kasha Shimmon was now retired and was spending his
sunset years in Urumia among his own people.[7] Sa'eed

---

[4]The Babis were the forerunners of the Bahais. Both religions
should be regarded as hereticial offshoots of Shiah Islam.
[5]A road has now been built around the mountain.
[6]Ps. 104:20, 22
[7]Kasha Shimmon died in July, 1918, at 104 years of age.

at once directed his course to his father-in-law's house, where he received a royal welcome. And wherever he went, he was affectionately spoken of as "Our Mirza Sa'-eed" or "Our Kurd."

Contrary to the method employed on his previous visits, Sa'eed felt led this time to devote his efforts especially to individuals. He definitely sought to avoid publicity. Great was the surprise of some of the ministers, therefore, when he declined their invitations to preach. But though he shunned the limelight, he sought to use every opportunity to reach individuals, whether man or woman, Moslem or Jew, nobleman or villager. He was an apostle of personal evangelism.

Some of the ministers were inclined to be skeptical of Sa'eed's efforts and critical of his teachings, regarding him somewhat unorthodox because he did not think just as they did nor share in their organized work. Even his father-in-law at first looked somewhat askance, but as he watched from day to day the devoted efforts to reach and help people and listened to his son-in-law interpreting the Scriptures, he was greatly touched. One day Kasha Shimmon confessed before a group: "We call ourselves the clergy and pass judgment on Sa'eed's work and say his views are unorthodox, but which one of us dares to contradict him, seeing that in everything he is wholly Scriptural? I confess that I have been cold in the service of the Master, but God has used the love and untiring zeal of my beloved son-in-law to humble me and provoke me to more whole-hearted devotion." Accordingly, on Sa'eed's subsequent visits to many villages on the Urumia plain the old pastor was a faithful companion.

One subject on which there was a wide difference of opinion was the acceptance of pay for religious work. Sa'eed had long since felt that he must be independent of any salary so as to avoid the stigma of having become a Christian for pecuniary reasons. Like Paul, he gloried in his freedom from outside support. On the other hand, the Assyrian pastors, in accordance with common usage throughout Christendom, received salaries from their churches or from mission funds. As a result, there was extended discussion over this moot question.

One day Sa'eed accepted a pressing invitation from Dr. Labaree of the Mission to meet some Bahai leaders, though he knew little good would result from argument. The Bahais started by asserting that their religion had superseded both Christianity and Islam and was superior to both. Little did they know with whom they had to deal! For five hours Sa'eed argued with them from the Bible, the Koran, and their own sacred book, now discoursing in the Turkish vernacular of that region, now quoting from the Arabic Koran or the Persian Bible. Before his profound knowledge they were dumbfounded. Suddenly he changed from argument to a passionate appeal to accept Christ as the only Savior. His sincerity and earnestness produced a strange effect on his hearers. They left, holding to their belief but quietly thoughtful.

After four months of this active work Dr. Sa'eed began to think of returning home. Letters from Hamadan reported the danger that awaited him. Upon request he had given a Hamadan mullah a copy of Dr. Tisdall's[8] *The Sources of Islam,* a book written by a British missionary in Iran which strikes at the very foundations of Mohammedanism by showing what elements in Islam had come from pre-Islamic Arabs, from the Old Testament and the Jews, from the New Testament and Christian heresies, and from Zoroastrianism, rather than being a direct revelation from God. This book had raised a furor. Some people had attributed its authorship to Dr. Sa'eed, saying "Tisdall" was only a *nom de plume* (from the Persian *teez del,* meaning "keen heart"). The leading ecclesiastic in Hamadan had issued a decree calling for Sa'eed's death. In spite of all this he decided he must return.

Sa'eed had urged the Christians in Urumia to send

_____
[8]The Rev. W. St. Clair Tisdall.

evangelists to Kurdistan, where he could not go. Dr. Jesse Yonan, his brother-in-law, who had just returned from medical studies in America, responded to the call. So they prepared to take the first part of the journey together. They left amid many tearful farewells from friends.

At their first stop a notorious brigand asked to call on them to obtain information about some of the diseases most prevalent in those parts. Arriving fully armed, he was offered the place of honor, but he seated himself nearer the door with his rifle across his knees. Noting Sa'eed's fluent use of different languages, he asked him to write something in each. The doctor gladly complied, writing John 3:16 in Persian, Turkish, Arabic, Kurdish, Syriac, and English and signing his name. "Sa'eed—why, that's a Kurdish name!" exclaimed the highwayman. The doctor explained that he was a Kurd, formerly a Moslem, now a Christian. A change came over the brigand's face as he grasped his rifle more tightly. Regretting that he had accepted Sa'eed's hospitality — for now he could not kill him — he rose and left.

In the village of Chayana the two doctors were guests at the home of Kasha Yohanan. The next day being Sunday, Dr. Sa'eed visited three Assyrian villages and exhorted the people to be firm in their faith. On Monday the pair departed on their way. It was the last time Sa'eed saw this beloved friend who had been the means of his conversion.

Before they left Urumia the doctors had been warned not to go through Saujbulagh, for report had it that two men from Senneh had made a special trip to that town with evil intent. The travelers were discussing what route to take, when Sa'eed abruptly turned to his companion: "All day yesterday we were exhorting the poor villagers to have faith in God's protective power, but now by our own doubts we are displaying our own lack of faith." At once they decided to go through Saujbulagh.

Even before reaching the town they were met by a

deputation from the Governor of the province, who proved
to be an old friend of Dr. Sa'eed and who invited the
travelers to be his guests. They sent the customary
greeting and asked to be excused. Instead, they went to
the home of Deacon Shmuel, the Christian evangelist
there. Soon after, servants from the Governor arrived
with two young lambs and other delicacies for their
evening meal, together with an invitation to dinner the
next day. They accepted and on arrival the Governor
embraced Sa'eed affectionately and kissed him on both
cheeks as an old friend. After an elaborate meal they
retired to the drawing room, where the guests were introduced to many of the high dignitaries of the province.

Many mullahs present were anxious to meet Sa'eed and
to hear from his own lips why he had left Islam. So the
following day was set for a meeting, at which he answered
all their questions with clear, uncompromising statements.
For an hour he spoke to them of the love of God as revealed in Christ. Some uneasiness was felt by a few who
recognized the two men from Senneh allegedly under a
vow to kill Sa'eed. At the close of the talk the pair
pushed forward. It was a tense moment. The assembled
group looked for some tragedy to be enacted. Instead, the
two men embraced Sa'eed. They were old classmates
from school days. Then a third man pressed forward
and clasped him in his arms. It was Mirza Hosein, his
patient of five years before.

"Friend," said Sa'eed, "do you remember you once
toyed with the temptation to kill me and warned me
never to set foot in Saujbulagh? Here is your chance."

Mirza Hosein hung his head and was silent for a
moment. Then he looked up: "I am ready to give my life
for you."

On the morrow about two hundred people came to see
the two doctors off. Four days later they reached Bijar,
where their ways parted, Dr. Yonan going to Senneh to
find rich experience in a new field and Dr. Sa'eed to

Hamadan, not knowing what the hostile fanatics of that city had in store for him. Two days later he entered the town at noon, the quietest hour of the day, to avoid as much as possible the gaze of unfriendly eyes.

What a joy to meet the family again after the absence of more than half a year! And what pleasure to hear the children's cries of delight over the toys he had brought from Urumia! The wind-up locomotives entranced not only the younger generation but the graybeards of the neighborhood as well.

CHAPTER SEVEN

Christian Witness Amid Intrigue

Despite all the feeling that was stirred up against Dr. Sa'eed during his absence, the first year or two after his return to Hamadan passed in comparative quiet. This was due in part to treatments in the homes of several important mullahs. The most celebrated ecclesiastic in Hamadan at this time was Abdul Majid, a Kurd who had spent many years at the famous schools of Shiah theology in Nejef and Kerbala, near Baghdad. His green sash-belt and dark turban marked him as a sayyid. He was renowned not only for his learning, but also for his strict observance of Islamic law. Once when a certain man had committed an act deserving capital punishment, this sayyid read the sentence of death before a large crowd and called for a volunteer to execute it. No one responding, he himself drew a sword and cut off the culprit's head.

In course of time Sayyid Abdul Majid fell seriously ill. The execution of the offender, though performed to up- hold the authority of Islamic law, preyed on his mind and added to his restlessness. His lack of confidence in the local physicians made him unwilling to consult them, but he finally agreed to send for Dr. Sa'eed. Examination showed advanced tuberculosis. All the doctor could do was to give him some medicine to relieve his cough. At the next call the sayyid looked very tired and complained of getting no rest.

"Why? Have you not taken the medicine?" asked Dr. Sa'eed.

"To tell the truth, no."

"Why not?"

"You have many enemies," the patient explained. "I was afraid the local practitioners out of jealousy would poison the minds of the people by saying, 'Sa'eed killed him with Ferangi drugs.' I thought I was dying anyway, so I wanted to spare you."

His words touched Sa'eed deeply. "I thank you for your consideration of me, but those who fear God will do what is right and leave the consequences with him."

The sayyid asked for the medicine and took a dose on the spot.

After a few weeks he died, but no one heeded the accusations, which were not slow in coming. His son remained a friend, gladly reading the New Testament given him, and came to understand much about Christian- ity.

One day Sa'eed called at the home of another sayyid friend and there he found four men discussing religion. In the course of the subsequent conversation, after one of the guests had accused Sa'eed of accepting Christianity for material advantages, the sayyid said: "That was my impression once, but I have been watching him for some time. Now I am of the opinion that he is a man who has found a heart-satisfying truth, so much so that he cannot

Dr. Sa'eed in 1903

listen to anything else. I think, however, that this is due to lack of deep searching in Islam." Then, turning to Sa'eed: "Apart from opinions gathered out of books have you yourself thought deeply about God in a passion to attain piety?"

The doctor answered with humility: "Yes, it was exactly that which made me seek after truth in my youth. The question with me was how a good God could accept a bad Kurd without blame attaching to his justice and with full assurance to my heart. In Christianity I found the answer. Had it not been so, why not remain a Moslem and avoid all the manifold troubles I have had to face?"

Thus it was that while Dr. Sa'eed had anticipated only trials on return from Urumia, he found great encouragement in the opportunities he found for bearing straightforward witness to his Christian faith before influential leaders of Islam and in their willingness to listen to him. Meantime, friends abroad, fearful of his continued safety in Iran, offered to settle the whole family in England, but Sa'eed's heart was in his own homeland, where he could render a far greater service to far needier people. The generous offer was declined.

In the spring of 1902 Dr. Sa'eed made another trip to London with the twofold purpose of putting Samuel, then nine and one-half years old, in an English school and of pursuing further medical study. Samuel was taken to live with the Warrens—in fact, it was they who had suggested his study in England — and they brought him up as their own son. The doctor was gone for about a year. He became a member of the London Polyclinic and took postgraduate studies in typology and bacteriology. He also devoted special time to ophthalmology and eye surgery. During his practice in Iran he had learned where he was weakest and so he concentrated on these phases of medicine, adding much to his knowledge and experience. He had an opportunity to hear a lecture on leprosy by Dr. Hansen of Norway, the discoverer of the leprosy bacillus, and was introduced to him by his old friend, Sir Patrick Manson.

The added experience gained by Dr. Sa'eed during this year of advanced study manifested itself in a series of brilliant cures soon after his return to Iran. His successes were proclaimed abroad, thereby increasing the jealousy of some of the local practitioners. In time he was summoned by the Governor, Prince Salar-es-Saltaneh, a son of Naser-ed-Din Shah and brother of the King, to treat his little boy, who was critically ill and had been given up by other doctors as a hopeless case. Success or failure was a matter of utmost importance to Dr. Sa'eed's future reputation. Eventually the boy made a complete recovery, filling the father's heart with deep gratitude and with admiration for the one who had effected the cure. Long nights of watching at the bedside of the young patient had given opportunity for much religious conversation, so that the Prince became well versed in Christian beliefs.

In the summer of 1904, when the hot season began, an epidemic of cholera broke out and soon had the city in tight grip. People were dying by the hundreds. The well-to-do fled to the hills or out-of-town resorts. Dr. Sa'eed was summoned to serve the Prince's household, camped for safety on the highest tableland of Mt. Alvand back of Hamadan, about 6,000 feet above the city. Some of the more common complaints of the encampment kept him busy, but he was able to make occasional visits to his own summer place, where eighteen families of Armenians and Jews were sheltered under Rebka's care.

Among the places that suffered most from the epidemic was the small village of Shavarin, about four miles to the northeast of Hamadan. Here, in his palatial residence amid costly rugs and candelabra with their glittering pendants, lived Amir Afkham, the wealthy feudal lord of the district. He owned many villages, where the underprivileged peasants, as all over Iran, plowed their fields with oxen, cut their wheat with sickles, threshed out the grain with ox-drawn, wooden-pegged rollers, winnowed it by tossing it in the breeze with primitive pitchforks, and shared the harvest, reaped in this backbreaking manner, with their luxury-loving landlord.

Despite his great wealth and power the Amir was disconsolate, for in the ladies' quarters his beautiful daughter lay dangerously ill with dysentery and in another room her mother, stricken with cholera. While Dr. Sa'eed was serving the Prince Governor in his mountain retreat, the Amir had no doctor of his ability to attend his sick wife and child. Although he knew of Sa'eed's accomplishments and was himself related to the Prince, he was not disposed to demean himself by asking the favor of the doctor's temporary release. He secretly harbored an intense dislike for the Governor, whom he accused of encroaching on his rights and attempting to curb his power. But as the two patients grew worse and friends urged on him the wisdom of summoning Sa'eed, he acquiesced.

Two weeks later a smile of satisfaction lighted up the Amir's face as he chatted happily with the doctor, who had been able to pull both patients out of the crisis. They were well on the way to recovery.

When Sa'eed returned to the Prince, he left his Armenian pupil in charge at the Amir's, promising to return if needed. The Amir often asked the young student questions about the Prince and his relations with Sa'eed. "Is he nearly a Christian now?" He laughed, then added: "It will take more than Sa'eed to convert our Governor. Perhaps sterner methods are needed. He has quite a way with us landowners, but we are not the kind of fruit you can squeeze easily. If you squeeze hard, the juice will squirt into your eyes." The student began to perceive what he meant, for he knew the Prince was disliked by the landowners.

With the coming of cold weather the epidemic subsided as mysteriously as it had started. People began to return to their normal occupations. In a few brief months ten per cent of the inhabitants of Hamadan had perished.

Once again Dr. Sa'eed resumed his practice in town, but from various quarters rumors of an ominous plot reached his ears. Soon rumor gave way to warning. Several friendly mullahs informed him that he had many enemies who were stirring the people up against him — "that vile man who never ceases to invite people to accept his religion." To all this Sa'eed turned a deaf ear. It had been long since the monster of persecution had raised its ugly head against him. The warnings became more insistent: "Leave town and save yourself before it is too late." One friend even urged him to get away that very night, assuring him that his enemies were bent on mischief. Sa'eed was puzzled and perturbed, but waited for God's guidance.

The motives behind this renewed outburst were two-fold—professional jealousy and political intrigue. On the one hand, Jewish practitioners, men who had given up their ancestral faith for Bahaism, envious of Sa'eed's successes, had placed Dr. Tisdall's *The Sources of Islam*[1] in the hands of some bigoted mullahs, attributing its authorship to Sa'eed. "Who but he knows all the languages quoted in it?" they argued — a sufficient proof for the fanatics.

On the other hand, if domestic discord could be stirred up, it would reflect on the Prince's firmness of control as governor. Secretly the Amir was hoping that the Governor, after a futile effort to put down the disturbance, would be obliged to tender his resignation. Thus Sa'eed became the innocent victim of political cunning and the jealousy of his fellow doctors.

The fanatical mullahs, headed by the Imam Jum'eh of the city, had gathered in the large central mosque and in secret session had signed a decree condemning Sa'eed to death for using blasphemous words against their Prophet and seeking to entice Moslems away from their faith. If read publicly in the mosque, this pronouncement, signed and sealed by the mullahs, would be the signal for the

[1]See page 92.

faithful to rise *en masse* to execute the sentence, on the authority of the Koran. The chief person responsible for the signing of the death warrant was none other than the son of the famous mullah of whom, on the day before he died, Sa'eed had inquired if he were not glad to go to meet God after so long a time of serving him.[2] That question had been asked many years ago, but apparently the confusion it had cost the father still rankled in the mind of the son. Later Sa'eed learned that this same man had played an important part in stirring up prejudice against him during his absence in Urumia.

The atmosphere of the city was tense. Rumors grew louder, like the rumbling of an earthquake about to burst forth. As anticipated by the Amir, the Governor was helpless in the situation, while he himself, through favors granted, had the mullahs on his side. With the storm about to break, involving the life of an innocent doctor who had saved his wife and daughter, the Amir was content to sit back on his soft cushions and smoke his water pipe with an air of amused satisfaction. On the other hand, the Governor already disliked for his overindulgence toward the apostate, dared not shelter him at this critical hour. Instead, he informed the Prime Minister of the situation by telegram.

At this juncture an escort arrived from the Amir to take Sa'eed and his family to Shavarin. Rebka flatly refused to go, saying no one would touch an old woman like her. The two children were taken away by friends and sheltered separately. Sa'eed left for the village under cover of darkness. Two days later his family followed him. In spite of strict orders, many of their belongings were lost during the move, even the servants taking their share of the loot.

Although the Amir now sought by all means in his power to quell the uprising, it looked as if the situation had passed the point of control. Sa'eed's whereabouts had become known. The Amir was in a difficult position.

---

[2]See page 84.

A band of theological students, headed by some fanatical merchants from Tabriz, together with hired assassins, set out for Shavarin to do away with the apostate. When news of this move reached the Amir, he immediately sent out two gray-bearded mullahs to intercept the mob and turn it back by any strategy they could devise. They swore by their Prophet and their holy Imams that Sa'eed had already left the village. Even thus it was only with the greatest difficulty that they accomplished their mission.

After this narrow escape for Sa'eed the Amir lost his habitual composure. He informed his guest that he could no longer shelter him, since he himself and his sons were being decried in the city for protecting "an enemy of the faith." "I have been in communication with the Prime Minister," he said, "and this is his reply." He handed a telegram to Sa'eed which read, "Send him directly to Teheran."

"The Prime Minister has always been very gracious to me," replied the doctor, "ever since I was called to treat his wife on their way to Kerbala.[3] Two years later I accompanied him to the south and remained in his service a whole year.[4] What he decides I am certain will be best."

When Sa'eed's friends learned of his decision to go to Teheran, they came from all over the city to say good-bye, for it was felt that he would be unable to return to Hamadan for some years. Rebka was not ready to go to the capital: she preferred to remain with their property in Hamadan. However, she made one concession: she promised to stay with friends for a while before returning home.

Among those who came to say farewell was a friendly mullah. On parting he said: "Well, doctor, are you going to continue to talk about Christ in Teheran also? Or have you learned your lesson?" Sa'eed assured him that his testimony would persist as long as he had breath.

---

[3]Kerbala is a Shiah shrine center near Baghdad.
[4]The Prime Minister at this time was Ain-ud-Dowleh. See page 88.

"Don't be surprised," the mullah said jokingly, "if the hounds follow the scent to Teheran." He bade the doctor an affectionate farewell.

Very different were Miss Montgomery's parting words: "God wants you to witness for him with power in Teheran. I am sure of it. Some day you will bear your testimony for him in your own home town in Kurdistan. I hope God will allow me to live to see that day." Her prophecy and her hope were both to be fulfilled.

It was on the first day of the new year that Dr. Sa'eed set out for Teheran. As he tore off the cover of his 1905 calendar, he found this as the Bible verse for the day: "For the Lord thy God bringeth thee into a good land. . . a land wherein thou shalt eat bread without scarceness, thou shalt not lack anything in it."[5] With a full heart he knelt with his wife and children to commend them to God.

Although the Amir wished to send an escort part of the way, Sa'eed preferred to leave as quietly as possible in order not to attract attention. With warm blankets, a hot water bottle, and a few necessaries packed in a bag, he rode out with his Armenian pupil and two servants of a friend to a village 20 miles away to catch the regular mail wagon. The temperature was below zero and the whole countryside was blanketed in a heavy frost.

As he started on the road, there came to him again the words that had been his help on his flight from Senneh to Hamadan: "There is no man that hath left house, or brethren, or sisters, or father, or mother, or wife, or children, or lands, for my sake, and the gospel's, but he shall receive an hundredfold now. . . with persecutions; and in the world to come eternal life."[6] He felt greatly comforted.

The Armenian often looked back to see if anyone were following, but no one came. "Do you know what happened in Shavarin two days ago?" he asked the doctor. Getting

5Deut. 8:7, 9
6Mark 10:29-30

a negative reply, he continued: "A young Armenian there got into trouble and to save his life proclaimed himself a Moslem. Our people were greatly upset and went to the Amir to get his help in reclaiming the fellow, explaining that he had become a Mohammedan through fear. You ought to have heard the Amir: 'Why are you so agitated over an idiot adopting Islam? Sa'eed, who is worth half of Islam, has gone over to your religion and we say nothing!' He literally pushed them out of the room, he was so angry."

On arrival at the post station the servants were dismissed. There were two other travelers besides Sa'eed and his companion in the heavily loaded, horse-drawn post wagon, one a cheerful young man and the other a Tabriz merchant, both of whom obviously did not know the doctor's identity. The only comforts along the road were the tea houses, where they could stop to get thawed out and Sa'eed could refill his bottle with hot water.

Their route lay by Sultanabad and Qom, the latter a shrine city with its tomb of Fatimeh, the sister of the eighth Shiah Imam. While they were waiting for mail delivery in Sultanabad, Sa'eed strolled to a nearby cemetery for quiet meditation. Of a sudden his gaze became fixed on a slab that bore the inscription, "Imam Jum'eh of Sultanabad. May the mercy of God rest upon him." Close by was a grave of more recent date, bearing the name of Sayyid Bagher. The Imam Jum'eh was the one who had led a band of theological students to Sa'eed's lodging fifteen years before to put him to death and Sayyid Bagher was one of the group.[7] Their plot had been foiled by his departure for Hamadan two hours earlier. Sa'eed could only thank God for his protecting care as the words of the ancient prophet came to his mind: "Whosoever shall gather together against thee shall fall for thy sake. . .No weapon that is formed against thee shall prosper."[8]

---

[7]See page 68.
[8]Isaiah 54:15, 17

As they approached the sacred city of Qom, the Moslem passengers began talking of their proposed pilgrimage to the shrine. In the midst of the conversation that had turned to religious subjects the merchant turned to Sa'eed: "By the way, what became of that apostate doctor in Hamadan who had written a book against Islam and created such an uproar?" The question was a bolt from the blue. There was no ignoring it. On the other hand, they were drawing near to a city whose shrine engendered fanaticism.

"I am Sa'eed, the apostate doctor."

The two Moslems gaped in astonishment.

"But I did not write the book in question." Then he went on to explain how the commotion had been caused by professional jealousy. His fellow travelers were quite satisfied. Three days beyond Qom, Sa'eed reached Teheran in safety.

On the following morning the allotted passage for his private devotions contained these words from the book of Acts: "Be not afraid, but speak and hold not thy peace: for I am with thee, and no man shall set on thee to hurt thee: for I have much people in this city."[9] He had many offers of hospitality, but, desirous not to bring trouble to any of his friends and anticipating the arrival of his family, he rented a house for two years. He signed the lease on the same day that he finished his reading of Acts, which concludes with these words: "And Paul dwelt two whole years in his own hired house, and received all that came in unto him, preaching the kingdom of God, and teaching those things which concern the Lord Jesus Christ, with all confidence, no man forbidding him."[10] This was exactly what he did.

Some days after his arrival Sa'eed went to pay his respects to his old friend, the Prime Minister, who welcomed him warmly and expressed relief at his safe arrival. After some conversation about details of health the Prime

---

[9]Acts 18:9-10
[10]Acts 28:30-31

Minister said: "Now tell me about yourself. They reported to me that you got drunk and blasphemed Islam. Of course I know you don't drink, but" — with a smile — "your blasphemous words I believe."

Sa'eed told him about his relationship with the Prince Governor and the Amir Afkham and the professional jealousies which had brought on the trouble. The Prime Minister smiled with amusement. "Do you know that your Governor has resigned?"

"Resigned?" asked Sa'eed in astonishment.

"Yes, he is in Teheran now. He foolishly sent in his resignation after you left. That is just what the Amir was aiming at. You and the Governor were the victims and the mullahs the instruments. The doctors were playing only a minor part in the game."

Sa'eed could hardly believe his ears. "Do you mean to say that the Amir was behind the whole affair?"

"Exactly! The Governor, like yourself, was innocent. He reported the situation to me at once. Later, the Amir sent me an account of the general disorder. I sensed what was up and telegraphed him, 'Let the doctor absent himself from town for a short time; meanwhile, if a broom is lost out of his belongings, I shall hold you personally responsible.' When the situation became serious, he sheltered you in his house and tried to silence the whole affair, but it got out of his control, though he did prevent the public reading of the decree. In desperation he asked by telegram what he should do and I ordered him to send you here."

And thus Sa'eed learned how he had been made the victim of political intrigue.

His next problem was to get his family to join him. He suggested to Rebka that she sell both house and country place and come to Teheran. She had no desire to do either. Finally they compromised. She agreed to go Teheran, but they would retain the property. In after years the wisdom of her decision was borne out when they returned to Hamadan to reside. The garden, especially, afforded them great peace and comfort when in later years they retired to its cool seclusion during summer months to find rest and joy in happy family reunions.

CHAPTER EIGHT

Among Nomads

The Kashgais are one of the great nomad tribes of Iran. Their homeland is in the south of the country in the province of Fars, whose capital city is Shiraz. They are reputed to have been transplanted from Kashgar in Chinese Turkestan in the thirteenth century by Hulagu Khan, grandson of Genghiz Khan. Of Turkish descent, Turkish had remained their spoken language, though in other respects they had adopted the habits of the neighboring tribes, the Lurs and the Bakhtiaris. Their warriors had accompanied Nader Shah on his invasion of India in the eighteenth century, when he brought back as his prize the famous Peacock Throne.

The Kashgai chieftain was known by the title of Ilkhani. His herds numbered literally hundreds of thousands of animals—sheep and goats, donkeys and camels. In the springtime he moved with his retinue of more than five thousand souls and his vast flocks toward

the north in the region of Isfahan, a trek that would take
several weeks. The fall saw this army moving back to
the pasture lands of the south. Over his subjects the
Ilkhani exercised absolute authority, and except in matters of taxation he enjoyed the powers and privileges of
a semi-independent chieftain. His people knew no other
authority and were accountable only to him.

In the fall of 1908 Dr. Sa'eed was requested to attend
the sick wife of this overlord at his summer headquarters
beyond Isfahan. Because of the length of the journey
and several patients under his care, he hesitated to accept,
but he was persuaded to call on the lady who was
arranging the trip. He was ushered into a drawing room
furnished in European style. Soon a lady of forty appeared, attired in European clothes except for a muslin
kerchief on her head, and she opened the subject. After
further conference with Rebka, who sensibly urged upon
him the need of a change of climate and living conditions,
Dr. Sa'eed decided to go. In a few hours everything was
arranged, including the employment of a young Assyrian
as a servant.

The party for the journey included nine persons — the
lady and her nephew, a woman companion and her
daughter of twelve, a maid and two men servants, the
doctor and his attendant. Travel was by three vehicles
—a wagon divided into two compartments by means of
boards and curtains, and two old-fashioned hacks. Huge
bundles of bed clothing, containers of food, and personal
baggage filled every available bit of space inside and out.
It was three hours past sunrise on a cloudless day when
they passed through the city gate into the open, dusty
country.

As the day grew warmer, the lady removed her jacket
and Sa'eed observed a revolver at her hip. Amused by
his surprised look, she asked, "How is it that you carry
no arms?"

"Once I had a revolver with me from Teheran to Hamadan," replied Sa'eed, "but I regretted it, for I found I

was relying on it in time of danger instead of looking to God for protection. I have never carried one since."

"That's all very well," she concluded. "Still we need to safeguard ourselves."

Their first main stop was Qom. For miles they had been passing caravans of pilgrims, many of whom were taking the bodies of their dead to ensure their eternal welfare by burial in the sacred soil of this holy city. The lady and her party found every caravanserai filled to capacity with these travelers. The only "hotel" was full; not only the rooms but also the flat rooftops were occupied. A little garden in front of the building was placed at their disposal and here Sa'eed found shelter in a sort of pergola. Her ladyship ordered everyone to go to sleep— a behest which the mosquitoes made difficult to obey— while she herself, rifle in hand, kept watch!

After a night in this city, near which one of the world's richest oil deposits has newly been opened, the party started on its way southward. The succession of mirages served only to intensify thirst, which was somewhat slaked by melons, but they could not take the place of fresh water.

At the next village the man charged with providing change of horses was slow and rude. The lady herself boxed his ears and ordered him whipped. Whenever the drivers or those responsible for bringing fresh horses proved troublesome, she attended to them personally. When at one station she found a jaded animal attached to her wagon, she threatened to shoot it: it was soon shifted. Even the rough men quailed before her. At sunset, as they were traveling through a mountainous section, she related to Sa'eed how one night she had helped a caravan through that very spot single-handed and had protected it against Lurish brigands.

At last the historic city of Isfahan and its magnificent Allah Verdi Khan bridge with its thirty-three arches came into view. At first Sa'eed was disappointed with the far-famed capital of Shah Abbas the Great, but when he reached the King's Square and saw the beautiful mosques and other witnesses to the city's ancient glory, he was happily surprised. Having visited the places of interest, he went to Julfa, the Armenian settlement outside the city, to secure a new supply of Scriptures and tracts.

From Isfahan Sa'eed went on without his feminine escort for a day's journey, when he was met by riders of the Ilkhani — a group of tall, well-built, broadshouldered men. Their leader, Iskandar Khan, a man of sixty, was as active as one half his age. A beautiful mare had been sent for the doctor's use.

An hour before midnight they set out for Shahneshin, the encampment of the great chieftain. The autumn air was icy cold. Across the plain small fires indicated sheltering tents, inviting to their hospitality, were it not for the loud barking of ferocious watchdogs. Some of the young men amused themselves by occasionally setting fire to camelthorn bushes. It was well past midnight when they halted at a small encampment of shepherds on the grassy slope of a hill. A huge fire was built for them. In spite of this Sa'eed could not sleep, his teeth chattered so from the cold.

An hour before sunrise they were again in their saddles. As they passed through peaceful villages, the Kashgais spread terror and confusion among the people, ordering them about like slaves to provide food and fodder with no compensation. Any hesitation was met with blows and curses. Two of the horsemen brought Sa'eed some food thus stolen, but he refused it because it was obtained by force. "O, this is not stealing; it was only fun," was the reply.

Suddenly the encampment of the Kashgais came into view—numerous black tents dotting the plain with one large white tent, the abode of the chief. Sa'eed was cordially welcomed by the Ilkhani, a tall, handsome, pleasant individual. He soon introduced the doctor to his patients — Bibi Khanum, his wife, and Naser, their boy of three. Both Bibi Khanum and her sister were beautiful ladies. The women here, as elsewhere among the nomads, wore no veils. They moved without embarrassment among the men. After a short rest in his own tent Sa'eed sent some presents to the Ilkhani and his wife, among other things a gilt-edged New Testament bound in leather.

One of his first concerns on arriving at the camp was to learn if the people could read. He was gratified to find that many were literate, both men and women. They could not read Turkish, their spoken language, but Persian, which most of them knew.

Among the dwellers at the camp was a remarkable young man, a sayyid called Bahr-ul-Olum (Sea of Knowledge), acting as personal physician to the chief. Sa'eed had never seen a man better versed in the Koran and Moslem traditions, in philosophy and metaphysics, in Arabic and Persian poetry — a lawyer in Islam and a doctor whose medical knowledge was remarkable for one who had acquired it only from books. This man was at first offended that another physician had been sent for. Sa'eed called on him. When he returned the call, Sa'eed was attending several patients in his tent. He explained their ailments to the sayyid. From then on he became Sa'eed's daily companion. He found it difficult to understand why the doctor was willing to share his medical knowledge. Sa'eed explained that it was to follow Christ's teaching, "Freely ye have received, freely give."[1]

One night the sayyid opened up his heart: "In spite of the books I have read, my critical mind has given me no rest. I have taught hundreds in Shiraz, being chief instructor in theology and metaphysics in Moshir's Mosque. I have found no satisfaction in Islam. Bahaism I have found shallow. Can't you tell me something? I know there is a God. I want to find salvation. You seem to be a strange Christian, so well acquainted with Islam and quoting the Koran with correct pronunciation."

---

[1]Mt. 10:8

Sa'eed told him who he was, and how he had come to accept the Christian faith, and what satisfaction he had found in it. The sayyid listened carefully and said he would like to read the Bible. The doctor's supply of Testaments was finished, so he wrote to Isfahan for an Arabic copy for the sayyid and, at his request, a Persian copy for his sister. To their mutual sorrow, the sayyid had to leave soon after for family reasons. Sa'eed's earnest prayers went with him.

The Kashgais are Shiah Moslems, but like most nomadic tribes they are not given to strict observance of Islamic practice nor imbued with devotion to the religious life. They maintain extreme veneration for Ali and corresponding hatred for Omar, the second caliph, who opposed him. Aside from these elemental traits of their faith they are governed chiefly by tribal traditions and concepts of right and wrong. Bravery is the paramount virtue and cowardice the cardinal sin. Tribal feuds are handed down from generation to generation.

As might be expected, the Ilkhani was not deeply interested in religion. One night he dropped in at Sa'eed's tent to find him engaged in discussion with his property overseer. He picked up the doctor's Bible with the remark, "I have been reading from the book you gave my wife, but I cannot understand it. It is unintelligible." As they carried on conversation, the Ilkhani was turning over leaves of the Bible. When he saw the Book of Job, he exclaimed, "O, Job! The Fountain of Job is in this district, where he is supposed to have bathed and was healed of his sores." Sa'eed related the story of Job, but the Ilkhani spoke sarcastically of the prophets.

Sa'eed cut him short: "What every man needs is a heart at peace before God. Will laughing at the prophets quiet your conscience? You are only a man. You may die tonight. Are you prepared to die?"

The Ilkhani sobered at once. After a pause he asked, "Do you have that peace you spoke of?"

"Thank God, I have," replied Sa'eed. The chieftain said goodnight and left.

The next day the Ilkhani came to Sa'eed's tent to express deep satisfaction with his wife's progress and to ask if she were now sufficiently recovered to ride, since he wished to commence the journey south to their winter quarters in Shiraz and further south near the Persian Gulf. When reassured of her condition, he volunteered to speak somewhat about her, revealing his deep attachment to her, not only for her beauty, but for her numerous virtuous qualities and fine character. She was indeed a clever and capable lady, attending personally to much that went on in the large household. Occasionally, even in her husband's absence, she ordered and provided food for five hundred guests. She seemed to know every article in her huge pavilion, which took thirty-two poles to pitch. In this enormous tent were beautiful rugs — two of them seven yards by three, trunks of valuables in the chieftain's quarters, looms for weaving carpets in the women's section. Every detail bespoke the orderliness and industry of its mistress.

By sunrise the next morning the whole camp was astir. Women were taking down the black tents, rolling them around their poles, and tying them on the backs of cows, donkeys, and mules. The grumbling camels were made to kneel for their loads, which might consist of tents, saddlebags filled with various articles, and a wooden chest on either side, the whole surmounted by one or more riders. When the load was complete, the animal would shoot his long neck forward with a sudden jerk, raise his hind legs and then his forelegs. Boys of eight or ten would perch on the camel's hind quarters without the aid of saddle or guide rope. Children of six or eight would ride horses, mules, or donkeys bareback. One might even see a camel's saddlebag loaded with four little children, two on either side, perhaps fast asleep with heads bobbing back and forth, the mother riding astride with another child in her arms.

Before setting out, the men lined up in rows to bow to
the Ilkhani. Not until he started did anyone move. They
were a magnificent sight, each one fully equipped and
riding a beautiful horse of Arab or Turkoman stock. Their
full-skirted coats were crossed over in front and held
together by massive sash-belts. Their full trousers were
of cotton material dyed indigo blue. A new German
Mauser pistol was slung over the left hip and a magazine
rifle across the shoulders. Woe to any enemy bold enough
to attack them!

By an hour after sunrise the entire camp was in motion.
The thousands upon thousands of camels and cows, mules
and donkeys, sheep and goats raised a dust that befogged
the plateau of sixteen square miles. They stopped for
lunch near the famous spring which Persian poets have
celebrated as the spot where the legendary romance of
Khosrov and Shirin occurred. Other springs below feed
into a brook which soon becomes a river. In springtime
grass and flowers touch a rider's stirrups and make one
of the best pasture lands in Iran, nearly 500 miles in
length. Even that year, at the end of a long dry season,
the nomads had to secure a guide to show them where to
ford the river. After he had crossed, none of Sa'eed's
companions would venture into the water until his pedi-
greed Arab horse had made the first plunge.

At one place a shepherd called to him. "What are you?
Why have you come to this region?" Sa'eed explained
that he was a doctor called by the Ilkhani to treat his
family. The man called two of his comrades. "If you are
a doctor, then tell us what's wrong with us."

"Physically, nothing; spiritually, sin, which brings you
under the judgment of God."

"Do you know God?"

"Yes, I rejoice to say."

"Then how is it you have such a hat?" referring to the
brim.

"That's to protect against the sun."

"Not so. We say you wear this to avoid seeing heaven, the abode of God." It was the same fanciful idea he had heard as a child in Kurdistan from his mother.[2]

Sa'eed greatly enjoyed watching the Kashgai men. On occasion one of these skilled marksmen suddenly would jump down from his horse, aim his gun, and bring down a bird, a hare, or a gazelle. One day the Ilkhani and his suite went hunting. They brought back fifty-four gazelles besides deer and mountain goats.

Although Sa'eed had seen difficult travel, he now came upon roads more difficult than he had ever known. Winding his way along a mountain ledge, he could see sheer cliffs reaching up into the sky, while a look over the precipice to the stream far below was enough to make him giddy. He found it both amusing and pathetic to watch the camels look at rocks in the road, smooth and slippery from weathering, dare to throw their front feet together, come what may; then wait, bewildered, wondering how to move their hind feet and where to put them. Horses also neighed in alarm. In such places the doctor thought it safer to walk, leading his mount.

One day the Ilkhani asked the doctor to see a patient, a man of eighty, who arrived with some young women and their husbands. The women asked if it were true that a Christian married only one wife. Sa'eed read some of the New Testament teachings regarding Christian marriage and family life. The women were astonished, but one husband said: "Please don't give them wings. They will become proud and haughty; then they will have to be beaten." Sa'eed wrote in a letter about these nomad women at the time:

"Poor women! With the exception of the higher class, they do everything—fetch skins of water, bake bread, and spin the thread: even while traveling she has the white wool over her head, and her hands are busy with the spindle. She pitches the tent, spreads the carpets, goes to the hillside and brings fuel for the fires, weaves carpets

---

[2]See page 23.

and the material for the large, heavy bags to carry provisions in.   She dyes the carpet yarns herself — all
beautifully matched. . .Practically everything is prepared
for her lord while he is gone shooting or on some duty
with the chief.   Often she is asked to saddle the horse too,
and when her lord is displeased, she is beaten.   Once I
thought a man was beating the dust out of a carpet, but
the shriek of a woman soon explained what was going on."

The Ilkhani's halts on the journey were frequent and
rather prolonged, since even he experienced some difficulty in collecting taxes from the various clans. Wherever
he stopped he held court, ordering punishments ranging
from a simple whipping to prison terms.   In his train
were to be seen in chains men guilty of various crimes,
being taken to Shiraz, where their fate would be determined.

At one of these stops Sa'eed discovered that the reputed
tomb of Job, which the Ilkhani had mentioned, was only
eight miles away, and so he asked permission to visit it.
The chieftain ordered a few riders to accompany him to
the locality, known as "The Land of Uz."   He found a
large graveyard surrounding a dome, beneath which was
the tomb — a little building of baked bricks with a
wooden box in the center, on which were lying a few
Arabic tablets, soiled and thumbed, and some prayers
read there by visiting pilgrims.   Removing the box with
the help of one of the men, he saw the grave, over which
was a piece of marble with an inscription which he was
unable to decipher.   On asking what proof there was that
this was the tomb of Job, the attendant adduced the fact
that worms from his body were still found there.   Sa'eed
asked if he could get some of these creatures.   The man
went off to a nearby hill and returned with some petrified
worms.

"How is it that the worms are confined to that hill?"
asked Sa'eed.

"Because when Job was in agony from his sores, he

used to go to that hill and roll himself in the dust to soothe his pain. As many worms as fell off were petrified!"

A three-day journey from there brought the long caravan to Shiraz. Here Sa'eed took his leave and set off by the mail wagon for Teheran. Two weeks later he reached the capital in safety, only to come down with an acute atttack of pneumonia. For a few days his condition was critical, but he made a complete recovery and was ready for further service with a deeper sense of God's sustaining power.

During the reign of Reza Shah the Ilkhani was confined in Teheran as a political prisoner. At his request Dr. Sa'eed attended him there daily in his last sickness. After his death it was widely reported that he was murdered. The doctor examined his body after decease and maintained that death was due to natural causes.[3] His oldest son — the little boy of three whom Sa'eed treated, grown to a young man in his twenties — succeeded his father as chief of the Kashgais.

---

[3]In his intensely interesting book, *Strange Lands and Friendly People* (Harper and Brothers, 1951), Justice Douglas states that he was murdered in prison by being given poisoned coffee (p. 134). Dr. Sa'eed's testimony would seem to disprove this.

CHAPTER NINE

In Senneh Again

The seven years of Dr. Sa'eed's residence in Teheran (1905-1912) were a busy time of growing practice, seeing patients from all classes — rich and poor, mullahs and sayyids, merchants and government officials. As in Hamadan, he carried on Bible readings in his home, attended at first only by Armenians, but gradually opened to Jews and Moslems. On the whole these were quiet years as far as his personal life was concerned. Persecution had abated.

During this period, however, Persia passed through an upheaval that changed the nation from an absolute to a constitutional monarchy. Mozaffar-ud-Din Shah—weak, prodigal, irresolute, and ailing—by his plundering of treasury funds and acquiring ruinous foreign loans raised such a bitter popular protest that he was forced in 1906 to grant the people a constitution. He died the following year and his son, Mohammed Ali Shah, succeeding to the throne, sought to restore the old order of things. New disorders broke out that resulted in his deposition and exile in 1909.

His son, Ahmad, only twelve years of age, assumed the rule under a regency. Within two years the ex-Shah, aided by royalist supporters, was moving from the Caspian Sea toward Teheran in the hope of regaining the crown, while his brother, the Salar-ud-Dowleh, was marching on the capital from the west with an army of irregulars, mostly Kurds and Lurs. The two brothers were trying to outrace each other for possession of the throne. The Salar took Senneh district without difficulty and by the summer of 1911 had reached the vicinity of Hamadan, where he received the support of Amir Afkham.

It was during this same summer that Dr. Sa'eed, together with Rebka and Samuel, back from London for the summer, went to their country place outside of Hamadan for a vacation. Sarah, their daughter, had been married three years before to Dr. Tatevos Assaturian, a prominent Armenian physician of Hamadan, where they were living. The news of the doctor's arrival soon reached the ears of the men who had sought his life six years before, but the lapse of time and the serious political crisis seemed to have moderated their religious fervor.

One afternoon a group of horsemen from the Amir arrived at Sa'eed's garden, begging him to come to Shavarin to treat his granddaughter's eye, injured accidentally by a toy gun. Remembering the Amir's perfidy, he was at first disinclined to go, but later yielded. Some days afterward Sa'eed received a telegraphic order from the Salar-ud-Dowleh to join his camp. Despite the fears of friends for the consequences, he refused. In the late summer both armies were defeated by nationalist forces and both brothers withdrew into exile. The Amir fled and his property in Shavarin was looted. He was eventually pardoned and returned to his village palace shorn of its glory. It was nearly two decades later that Dr. Sa'eed was summoned to his deathbed. It was a pathetic ending to the years of acquaintance to hear the dying man cry out from the sting of a troubled conscience, "God will take vengeance! God will take vengeance!"

Of the royalist captives taken to Teheran many were Kurds, among them some from Senneh who had once vowed to kill Sa'eed and many from Awraman, a district near the Turkish border. It was from this region that Sa'eed's mother had come as a bride to Senneh long years before. The doctor, now returned to the capital from his vacation, visited many of these prisoners, treated the wounded, and gave some of them money. He was able through his great influence to obtain the release of many, whom he sent back to their homes. They returned to Kurdistan with unbelievable stories about the apostate doctor. "He works miracles!" said some. "I was one of the men who swore to kill him," said another, "but he cured my eyes, gave me money and clothing, and sped me on my way home!"

Such were the reports borne to the Sultan of Awraman, an influential chieftain of that district. He was now seventy-two years of age. For nearly four years he had been blind. Through this dark period he had been hearing of Sa'eed's medical skill and he cherished the hope that some day, somehow, the doctor would come and restore his sight. He had given the Salar generous support in men and money and in return asked one favor only—that he would send Sa'eed to operate on his eyes. The Salar's defeat had shattered his hopes and brought bitter disappointment.

In the summer of 1912 Dr. Sa'eed returned again to Hamadan, this time for permanent residence. Naser-ul-Molk, a European-educated nobleman, was acting as regent for the young king. He was not the strong man needed to bring order out of chaos and as a result disorder and lawlessness prevailed in many parts of the country. Roads were unsafe for travel. Sa'eed's trip from Teheran was accomplished with difficulty; though shots were fired on his carriage, he reached Hamadan in safety.

Toward the end of September he was summoned to Khosrovabad, a village on the border of Kurdistan, to treat a nobleman of repute, Amir Ala-ed-Din. With an escort of six armed riders and two servants sent by the Amir, Sa'eed set out, taking his own Kurdish servant, Bagher. The Amir, one of the savants of his day famed for his beautiful penmanship, was suffering from mental decline following inflammation of the brain surface. By producing artifical fever the doctor was able to secure extraordinary results in a short time. The improvement was so marked that his own sons said, "The Amir reads and writes as he used to twenty years ago!"

Because of this success the Amir became so attached to Sa'eed that each time he asked permission to leave some excuse was found to detain him. Meanwhile many patients came from neighboring villages for treatment and were cured.

Toward the middle of October came a letter from Amruleh, a village in Kurdistan, requesting Dr. Sa'eed's presence. The missive was from Sayyid Najm-ed-Din, a noted man who had followers from the Caspian basin to the distant mountains of Kurdistan and who controlled a monastery of great repute. He wrote to ask the doctor to come to treat a relative. Sa'eed thought it unwise to venture among the fanatical Moslem leaders of that Kurdish district. His friends at the Amir's advised against it. One in particular emphatically warned, "Don't ever let such an idea enter your head. You would be killed outright." So the doctor replied to the sayyid, asking to be excused from making the trip.

The messenger who carried the letter was caught in a rainstorm on his way back and was drenched to the skin. Seeking shelter in the nearest nomad tent, he at once set about drying himself. In the process the doctor's letter dropped into the open fire and was burned to ashes.

A week passed, during which Sa'eed persistently sought to return to Hamadan, but was daily hindered by the Amir's devices to delay him. As a result, another letter arrived from Sayyid Najm-ed-Din:

"We did not see your letter and have no idea of its contents, for it was accidentally burned on the way. I hope you did not intend to disappoint us. I am a man who may request any favor from the Sultan of Turkey or the Shah of Persia and am not refused. I have received a letter from the Sultan of Awraman. He wishes to come here to Amruleh and wants you to treat his eyes. Be sure to come."

So it was the blind Sultan of Awraman behind this! What should he do? He did not have the heart to refuse the old Sultan of his people, nor did he deem it sensible to throw himself into the lions' den. Did God have some purpose in the burning of his letter? He was greatly perplexed. One of the Kurds at the Amir's suggested a solution — that he demand a fabulous fee and perhaps that would discourage the Sultan. So he wrote, saying he would come for fifty tomans a day from the time he left Khosrovabad till the time he should return there.

When the time limit stipulated in his letter had expired and no reply came, Sa'eed, relieved, set out for home. On the way he stopped at a small village to return the call of a nobleman friend of his childhood days who had come to see him in Khosrovabad. The preparation of a sumptuous repast delayed the doctor's departure till two o'clock and even before the meal was over, patients began to arrive.

Before Sa'eed could get away, the clatter of hoofs announced the arrival of Sayyid Jalal-ed-Din, the son of Najm-ed-Din, at the head of a large escort armed with daggers and pistols, rifles and cartridge belts. Sa'eed's host rushed forward to kiss the sayyid's stirrup and receive him with the honor due his position. To everyone's astonishment Sa'eed greeted him with only a bow and the customary salutation. The sayyid handed him a

letter from his father promising him any fee he should
wish. They all spent the night there, but Sa'eed slept
little, for he was greatly disturbed at the way things had
turned out.

The next day they returned to the house of the Amir
in Khosrovabad. Before they had time to dismount,
Sa'eed was greeted with these words: "What do you
think has happened? This morning some ten letters
arrived for you from Senneh. They want you urgently
to treat our Governor the Vakil-ul Molk." The letters
were from the Governor himself and several of the
aristocracy of Kurdistan. The Governor had also written
the Amir:

"I know there would be danger for the doctor to come
to Senneh. It would be best for him to proceed to one of
my villages near the town. Though I am not in a position
to travel I shall arrange to meet him for examination and
directions."

This latest development added a new twist to the riddle.
Here were two calls for his help — one from his native
city, the other from the mountain fastnesses of Kurdistan,
both from fanatical centers, both from important men and
men at odds with each other. More perplexed than ever,
Sa'eed sought seclusion to secure guidance from God. He
felt encouraged to accept both calls. As he came out of
his room, he said to his servant, "What do you say?"

Bagher replied, "The God whom you worship in truth
is able to protect you even in the burning fire."

Turning to the sons of the Amir, Sa'eed said: "I came
here in the first instance at your father's behest. If you
see any danger in all this, why should I leave your house?"
As a result of this remark the young men held a long consultation with Sayyid Jalal-ed-Din, for they felt responsible for Sa'eed, since he came there to treat their father.
The upshot of their deliberation was that Jalal-ed-Din
gave a written guarantee for the doctor's safe return to
their home, once the whole undertaking was completed.
So Sa'eed wrote a letter to the Vakil, promising to come

to Senneh, for from the description of his ailment it seemed unwise for him to be moved, and asking for an escort to meet him in Amruleh.

With a heart full of diverse emotions the doctor set out with Sayyid Jalal-ed-Din and his men. Wherever they passed people rushed forward to kiss the sayyid's feet, so great was the veneration in which he was held. Toward sunset of the third day they arrived at Amruleh, where the sayyid's father had his great monastery. This was the village where it was agreed that the Sultan of Awraman should come for the treatment of his eyes and where the Vakil's escort should meet Sa'eed for the trip to Senneh, but there was no sign of either party.

Sa'eed was assigned to a room whose walls were blackened with the smoke of years and bespattered with the spittle of numberless pilgrims who had visited the sacred place. He sent his servant to the bazaar to buy some yards of calico to nail on the walls and on the corner of the room where he slept as a precaution against lingering germs.

At dusk a deputation from Awraman came riding in. Jalal-ed-Din went out to meet them and report.

"Well, has the Sultan come?" asked Sa'eed.

"No. You see he is very fat as well as blind. Travel over these mountain roads would be very difficult for him. He begs you to go to him."

"But that is impossible." The doctor shook his head.

About three o'clock in the morning Bagher burst into Sa'eed's room. "Sheikh Sadeq is suffering from a severe pain. They want you to see him." The sheikh was one of the Awraman contingent just arrived.

A careful examination showed unmistakable signs of appendicitis. The doctor groaned: "What a beginning is this for me? No instruments! No anesthesia! No assistant! This is my undoing. If anything should happen to this influential man, I would be ruined." Much against his better knowledge he injected the patient with mor-

phine to ease his pain, forbade all food, and ordered cold
compresses over the appendix. He returned to bed with
a prayer to God to heal the man, since an operation was
impossible. In the morning he found the patient breath-
ing at ease with all pain gone. Re-examination showed
no trace of the disease. Sa'eed's reputation was saved.
In fact, it was enhanced. He thanked God in the words
of the Psalmist: "This poor man cried and the Lord heard
him, and saved him out of all his troubles."[1]

After this Dr. Sa'eed was invited to call on Jalal-ed-
Din's father, Sayyid Najm-ed-Din, who received him in
a huge audience hall packed with dignitaries and at-
tendants. Although he refused to kiss the great man's
hand as a sign of reverence, as others did, lest the people
should construe it to mean that he had repented of his
apostasy, the venerable ecclesiastic seated him at his side.
Then they acquainted him with their plan, which was
that he should go to Awraman to treat the Sultan's eyes.
They urged, they flattered, they pleaded.

Sa'eed was hard pressed. "I have no instruments,
should an operation prove necessary. You had better
bring the Sultan to a village here for me to examine him.
If he can be cured, I will take him to Hamadan to be
treated there." Their reply was to offer him fifty tomans
as the first day's fee to go to Awraman!

"Gentlemen," he finally said, "I have promised Vakil-
ul-Molk to go to Senneh and today his escort will be
arriving. If they come, I shall go with them. After that
I shall go to Awraman, providing that Sayyid Jalal-ed-
Din will accompany me there and back according to his
written guarantee."

The Awramis said: "Of course Jalal-ed-Din will go
with us, but we hope to God the Vakil is dead by this time
and no one will turn up to take you!"

"Would you like the people of Senneh to pray likewise
for your Sultan?"

[1]Ps. 34:6

"No!"

"Then why do you consider it right to wish death for someone else?" There was no answer.

Soon afterward the Vakil's riders were heard arriving. This threw confusion among the Awramis, especially when they saw Sa'eed preparing to go with them. After they had consulted together, Jalal-ed-Din took the doctor aside. "They all beg you not to go to Senneh."

"How can I break my word? I have promised to go."

"They offer you a hundred tomans not to go."

"My word of honor is worth more to me. Please do not insist."

"They will give you two hundred." Sa'eed shook his head.

"Three hundred."

"Even if they offer me three thousand, I will refuse. Truth and integrity are more precious to me than money. But just as I gave my word of honor to the Vakil, so I promise that after I have treated him I will go to Awraman."

Since there was bad feeling between the Awramis and the people of Senneh over some property matters, the Sultan's men were ready to fall on the Vakil's deputation and take Sa'eed by force. Seeing this, Jalal-ed-Din rebuked them sharply: "You wish to take the doctor to Awraman to treat the eyes of your Sultan. What sort of encouragement is this you are giving him? You had better accept his promise and leave it at that." His words saved a clash.

The next morning Sa'eed and his escort set off for Senneh. Unknown to him the Awramis had given Bagher a sealed bag containing three hundred tomans to put in the doctor's baggage as an earnest to assure his keeping his promise to go to Awraman!

Three hours before sunset Senneh appeared in the distance. What a flood of memories surged through Sa'-eed's mind! Even now he was on the very hill from which thirty years before he had taken his farewell look at his native city, which he never expected to see again. There was the meadow where he and his schoolmates often went for a picnic lunch. Farther north was the desolate cemetery where his parents were buried, and close by the leper colony which he had visited with his father. Every familiar spot spoke volumes to him.

As he passed the cemetery, a few mullahs were teaching the catechism to some people newly buried.[2] He remembered his host of the night before, the headman of the village. When the man said his evening prayers, instead of using the prescribed words, he repeated one phrase over and over again, while going through the proper movements. When Sa'eed asked him the reason for this unusual procedure, he explained that, try as he would, he could not memorize the Arabic words, and a mullah had told him to repeat this phrase instead and God would accept it. Sa'eed now thought to himself: "Poor Kurd! You could not learn your Arabic prayer when you were alive; but when you are dead, they will expect you to learn your catechism in that same language!"

As they approached the outskirts of the city, the head of the escort drew up to say that he had strict orders from the Governor to enter the town by a circuitous and less frequented route leading to his residence. To Sa'eed this seemed cowardly and unworthy of a Christian. As he prayed in his heart, there came to him the words of Nehemiah, "Should such a man as I flee?"[3] Thereupon he said to the chief of the escort, "We shall proceed right through the town."

"I shall be held accountable if anything happens," protested the other.

"It will not affect you. I shall be responsible for my own action."

---

[2]See page 20.
[3]Neh. 6:11

With that they rode along the wide avenue leading through the center of the city to the Governor's mansion. They went through the crowded bazaars, by the houses of the nobility, past the monastery where he had studied the mystical theology of the Naqshbandis, until at last they reached their destination. All along the way instead of threats there were shouts of "Welcome back!" Shopkeepers eagerly spread the news from one to another: "Yes, it is Dr. Sa'eed! He has come to treat our Vakil." Some uncovered their heads[4] as he passed, saying, "*Insha'ullah* (God willing), your return to us will be blessed!"

Various tests showed the Vakil to be afflicted with chronic nephritis. He was also suffering from severe headache due to high blood pressure. An injection of a sweat-producing drug and a hot bath relieved both pressure and headache, so that the next day he was much better.

As Sa'eed read his Bible that morning, his eyes fastened on the words "Call unto me, and I will answer thee, and shew thee great and mighty things, which thou knowest not."[5] How wonderfully his welcome to his native city after thirty years had fulfilled this saying! With a glad heart he showed the verse to the Governor.

Soon word came that a crowd of patients was waiting to see the doctor. The Vakil, fearful lest some people bent on mischief should pretend to be sick, thought to turn them away, but Sa'eed said he would be glad to see them and leave the result to God. He set up his clinic on a huge porch facing the east, from which there was a beautiful view of the whole city. In the distance could be seen the stream over which Kaka had carried him on that memorable day of his flight. A kind of seat was

---

[4]This custom of removing the hat, unknown to other Islamic peoples, is frequently practised in Kurdistan. It is a sign that a man wishes to offer his heartiest prayer. It was Dr. Sa'eed's conviction that once the Kurds were Christians and he thought that this and other practices confirmed his belief.

[5]Jer. 33:3

improvised for the doctor and the patients were admitted
a few at a time. He treated them all without charge.
Unknown to him, sitting behind him on the stone balus-
trade of the balcony, on order of the Governor and with
a revolver in his hand, was the chief of the escort ready
to defend him if necessary!

Dr. Sa'eed one day expressed a wish to visit some of his
old haunts. The men of the Vakil's·household, ever mind-
ful of his safety, accompanied him personally. They
visited the old homestead, now in ruins, saw the Catholic
church so replete with the memories of the beloved
Mar Shimmon, passed the mosque where he used to give
the call to prayer and finally sought the resting place of
his parents at the cemetery, where in a few moments of
silence he relived his whole life. He returned both sad
and happy, grateful to God that after three decades he
had been permitted to visit his native city once again.

After five days the Governor's condition was greatly
improved. Detailed instructions for his future care were
given the eldest son, a member of the Mejlis (Parliament)
in Teheran, and he was warned of possible danger. During this brief period many were the sick that Sa'eed
helped and many the prominent people that came to call
on him, some from friendliness, some from curiosity.
Letters came from Hamadan; friends rebuked him for his
folly, but Rebka appeared to be taking the situation
philosophically. Miss Montgomery was rejoicing that
her prophecy that he would some day visit Kurdistan
again was at last fulfilled.

The friends, one and all, including the Governor, sought
to dissuade the doctor from going to Awraman, fearing
that the trip of an apostate to such a fanatical district
was fraught with too much danger. Numerous stories
were related to him about the notorious faithlessness
of the Awramis, how they would swear fidelity on the
Koran, only to stab one in the back a moment later.
Suppose he should fail to cure the Sultan's eyes, then
what? One friend especially, a poet, remained with him

all the last night, hoping to deter him from going. His first words in the morning were, "I hope you have decided not to go."

"On the contrary," said the doctor, "I have resolved to go."

"But you will be killed."

"Then they will say, 'He was killed while trying to keep his word.'"

A horse was prepared for him at sunrise. The Vakil's oldest son, a friend of many years, accompanied him to the gate. With deep feeling he said, "I trust the Lord will protect you." With this parting word the doctor and his escort were off.

CHAPTER TEN

On to Awraman

From the Vakil's house to the village where the Awramis were waiting Dr. Sa'eed was accompanied by a venerable sayyid with a massive green turban and a long gray beard. A few others went along. Though the people of Senneh feared that he was going to his own slaughter, Sa'eed was happy to be keeping his plighted word.

The Awramis were delighted to see him. Their first words were, "Did they not try to dissuade you?"

"To a man," replied the doctor.

Singing and laughing, the escort mounted their horses for the arduous trip to the mountain country. Sayyid Jalal-ed-Din, the guarantor of the doctor's safety, was absent: they explained that he had gone to the tax office to settle some business and would soon catch up. As they rode along, the scenery seemed familiar to Sa'eed. Suddenly it dawned on him: this was the very road he had traveled with his father at the time of the famine forty years before, when he was a little boy of nine.

After riding for some distance the escort stopped to await the arrival of Jalal-ed-Din. When he finally drew up, they were obviously relieved. Two years later Dr. Sa'eed accidentally learned that he had not been to the tax office at all, but because the Awramis in Salar-ed-Dowleh's army had pillaged this district the year before and had massacred some of the inhabitants, the people were waiting for a chance to retaliate. Jalal-ed-Din had gone to beg them in the name of his father to do nothing at this time. "I am responsible for the doctor's life," he told them. "If a hair of his head is touched, the English will come and take away even the soil of this land in sacks. Leave your revenge for another time." With such dire threats he had averted a possible attack.

On the next day as they traveled in the Awrami territory, the mountain paths were so narrow that the slightest slip would have hurled both rider and mount into a ravine of jagged rocks hundreds of feet below. But the horses, born and bred in these highlands, were surefooted and managed to negotiate the dangerous ledges. At one place the doctor lost his nerve and, dismounting, crossed a difficult passage on his hands and feet! When at last they reached the top of this ascent, he could see the majestic Shahoo and other cragged peaks of Awraman clad in their mantle of white.

For lunch they halted at a small village where there were ruins of great antiquity. Sa'eed had learned of the existence of an ancient copy of the Koran written on parchment and kept in the local mosque. This famous antique he was permitted to see. He also procured the manuscript of an old poem dating from 80 B.C. It is now in the British Museum.

When the people of Razab, the Sultan's village, saw the cavalcade approaching, some of the important men, following Persian custom, went out to meet the travelers.

As they wound up the hill to the Sultan's residence, a crowd followed. On the entranceway leading to the mansion had been stretched a roll of calico. At the end of this cloth pathway was spread a beautiful rug, on which the blind Sultan was standing to receive his guest. Sa'eed refused to ride or walk over this carpeting, for he did not feel worthy of a reception accorded only to the highest. Instead, he dismounted and respectfully saluted his host, but the Sultan embraced him and kissed him on both cheeks in Persian fashion, expressing his gratitude for making the hazardous trip on his account.

It being toward sunset, Sa'eed was conducted to the guest house, accompanied by the watchful Jalal-ed-Din. After a brief rest the doctor took his ophthalmoscope and called on the Sultan for an examination. His discoveries were disheartening. Both eyes were diseased with trachoma. Worse than this, the left eye had been operated on two years before by an incompetent oculist with resultant secondary glaucoma accompanied by long and painful headaches. The pressure in the right eyeball was also pronounced. As if this were not enough, further physical examination in the morning revealed other symptoms in this seventy-two-year-old patient. Moreover, he was a diabetic. In short, everything was against . an operation.

"What result?" asked Jalal-ed-Din, as he found the doctor depressed.

"Hopeless!" He described the situation briefly and arranged with Jalal-ed-Din to approach the Sultan with the sad verdict and ask for permission to leave. Sa'eed was disconsolate and extremely sorry for the poor old man to be thus disappointed after long years of expectancy, but there seemed to be no other solution. Both medically and ethically an operation was out of the question.

Poor old Sultan! He said bravely: "I have fallen a prey to my enemies' mockery. They will rejoice in Senneh. For years I have waited for this day. I have employed a thousand tricks to get Sa'eed here to cure me, and this is what he says." With a pathetic plea he held the hem of Jalal-ed-Din's mantle: "Give him everything I possess. Only let me see through this eye that has not been operated on. I ask for nothing else."

Jalal-ed-Din reported what the Sultan had said. Sa'eed again explained how dangerous the operation would be under the circumstances and concluded: "I fear such a procedure would subject the Sultan to more headache and pain. I have no desire to cause him more suffering and ruin my own reputation at the same time."

The Sultan was resigned to the verdict. It was arranged that the doctor should leave for Senneh in the morning.

That night, as Sa'eed read his Bible, the passage was the eleventh chapter of the Gospel of John — the story of the raising of Lazarus. Each word seemed to glow with a new light. It was as if he could hear the voice of God speaking to him in unmistakable words: "Behold the One who never used such terms as 'perhaps,' 'maybe,' 'possibly,' who never said a word or took a step of which he afterwards repented! This Person hears that his friend is dangerously ill. He is obedient to his Father's will, not to human thoughts. He says so long as the light shines on the path of duty, he will go, even though the Jews were preparing to kill him. Human wisdom at once raises the standard of alarm and tries to stop him from going, but on learning the will of the Father, he brushes aside all human caution and goes forward with steadfast step. Think and remember: Have I not guided you at every stage of the way since the beginning of this trip? Have I not proved to you again and again that it was my will you should make this journey? I have protected you from all harm. I have sent you to this old man, who has been calling to me for four years, 'Send me Sa'eed to cure my eyes.' But you, without accomplishing your duty, are deserting him. You trust your knowledge rather than me, forgetting that I am the God of resurrection, for whom nothing is impossible."

In humble adoration Sa'eed answered: "I obey, my Lord, thou God of resurrection. In thy hands I gladly leave the results." As a perpetual reminder of this experience he wrote the date — Nov. 13, 1912 — at the head of this chapter in his Bible.

In the morning, when Jalal-ed-Din came to say that the horses were being saddled, Sa'eed announced that he was not going. Surprised, the sayyid asked why. "God does not permit me to go," replied the doctor. "I shall stay and perform the operation. Go and ask the Sultan for a man to take my telegram to Senneh to be sent to Hamadan for my instruments." Then he added, "Lest the Sultan think I have been holding off for money, tell him he can pay me whatever he wishes. I am remaining in obedience to God and my trust is in him."

The Sultan was overjoyed. The telegram was sent. It would be at least a week before the instruments could arrive.

During this interval the Sultan's eyelids were cauterized and he was put on a strict diet, as a result of which his general condition improved considerably. A special room was selected for the operation. As in most village houses, the flooring had been made of mud mixed with straw and smoothed over with a mason's trowel. Anyone walking over it could easily stir up dust. The plastered walls were safe. The roof had been made of poplar beams set on the walls a foot or so apart. Over these had been placed coarse matting, covered by a layer of brushwood and camelthorn packed in with earth and that in turn overlaid with a heavy coat of mud plaster, which had dried and hardened in the sun. Particles dropping from such a ceiling could easily be a source of infection. So calico was nailed to both floor and ceiling as a sanitary precaution.

The following Friday was tentatively set for the ordeal. Meanwhile, a crowd of people suffering from all kinds of ailments came streaming into Razab for treatment. All day long from early in the morning Sa'eed was busy seeing patients and in the evening he was busy preparing medicines or boiling gauze and instruments. Besides this, many of his relatives came to call.

One of these, a cousin who once had been his tutor, now an accomplished mullah, came with several friends. He expressed pleasure at reunion and hoped that Sa'eed would return to the fold that he had mistakenly abandoned in his youth. His patronizing attitude somewhat irked Sa'eed and provoked him into replying: "Cousin, you are now sixty years of age. You have made the pilgrimage to Mecca and Medina. After all this do you have the assurance of acceptance by God? Suppose you were to die tonight: are you sure you would go to Paradise?"

"No. But who can be sure?"

"Haji,[1] a religion that gives me no assurance of salvation I wouldn't buy for a farthing." This was a bold reply. The mullah and his friends looked at one another, but made no further comment about Sa'eed's "mistake."

On one of these days of waiting Dr. Sa'eed received a request from Sheikh Ala-ed-Din to come and see his daughter, who was ill. The sheikh was an influential and crafty ecclesiastic living near the Turkish border. He was a master hand at deceiving the simple village folk around him, but the higher classes knew him for the wily man that he was: in fact, they nicknamed him Bala-ed-Din. (Ala-ed-Din means Grandeur of the Faith, Bala-ed-Din, Pest of the Faith.) Two years before he had given help to the Salar-ed-Doweh at the time of his abortive attempt to seize the throne and had personally set out toward Hamadan under solemn oath to kill Sa'eed and rid the Kurds and Islam of the shame of his apostasy. Despite this the doctor decided to go. The Sultan gave him six riders to accompany him.

Upon arriving at the sheikh's village Sa'eed found him in a big audience room with some forty notables and

---

[1]Title of one who has made the pilgrimage to Mecca.

followers seated in a large circle. Sa'eed went forward to greet the sheikh, but he remained seated, expecting the doctor to bend over and kiss his hand. This Sa'eed refused to do, so the sheikh arose and motioned him to a seat beside himself. After the customary salutations Sa'eed said, "If you have no objections, I should like to see the patient, since I have work in Razab and must return soon."

"Shall we not have lunch first?" asked his host.

It soon became evident that he had made extensive preparations to beguile his guest. He had invited dervishes and musicians to provide an atmosphere. These now began moaning and groaning and uttering prayers to the plaintive sound of the flute and the beat of tambourines, while they fixed their gaze on the apostate, whom they sought by these means to mesmerize to penitence. Such methods are often employed for the reclamation of a disaffected individual. They recited poems, they repeated the names of their leaders, and some roared like wild beasts. By these agencies they hoped to cast a hypnotic spell over Sa'eed to the weakening of his will power. On the contrary, it made him think of the prophets of Baal in their contest with Elijah.[2] It humbled him to recall that he had once been such as these. In his heart he thanked God that he had been called out of darkness into light.

After lunch he accompanied the sheikh to the ladies' quarters to see his daughter, a young lady famous for her beauty. Though she was heavily wrapped, the doctor managed to examine her quite thoroughly, while the sheikh watched with eagle eye. After they left, he gave his verdict: "Your daughter is a consumptive. She will be your guest and her husband's for only a year." The sheikh was grief-stricken.

Four years before Sa'eed had heard that some ancient documents on parchment had been found in a cave near here and turned over to Sheikh Ala-ed-Din; that he had

---

[2] I Kings 18:25-29

sent them to Senneh to find someone who could read them, but in vain; and that they were subsequently returned to him. Sa'eed had written several times to Senneh for information about these manuscripts, but without getting any satisfaction. Now he had a chance to ask the sheikh himself. He learned that only three sheets of the parchment had been preserved and that these had been given to the Salar-ed-Dowleh at his request. Sa'eed was greatly disappointed.

He now set out to return to Razab, but a message from the sheikh soon overtook him with a request for a second examination of his daughter: "Maybe your first findings were not correct, but another checkup in this place would not be free from risk, since I have heard some people intend mischief." He named another village nearby. The doctor accepted, but he could only report that the second examination confirmed the first. A year later the accuracy of his verdict was borne out by her death.

No sooner had Sa'eed returned to the Sultan's house than the stream of patients resumed its flow. The day set for the operation finally dawned. The instruments had come from Hamadan. The Sultan requested that the hour be postponed until Sheikh Ala-ed-Din should arrive. The late November days were short and it was late when he finally put in appearance. He and a few of the Sultan's intimates crowded into the small room prepared for the occasion. Sa'eed begged them to be quiet so as not to stir up dust. Even as he started to work, the light began to fade, a cloud coming over the sun. The Sheikh ordered servants to bring the Sultan's huge mirror to reflect light on the field of operation.

Since the conjunctiva was ruined, the doctor had to hold it delicately with forceps to avoid tearing. When his knife reached the corneal junction it seemed blunt. Carefully he retracted it to insert a second — a dangerous procedure — but this seemed no sharper. On account of the glaucoma, the patient's advanced age, and the long use of caustics and astringents, the cornea had become a horny mass. With a quaking heart he cut with a to-and-fro motion, or as he himself said, he "actually tore." By now the room was in twilight. As he wrote later, "I had no faith in my instruments or my skill, but my trust was in Him who raiseth the dead." When he attempted an iridectomy, the iris literally fell to pieces, it was so lifeless. He cut the lens loose from its moorings and removed it. Both he and the Sultan were relieved that the latter could count the doctor's fingers as a preliminary test. He finally closed the eye with instructions that it remain shut for four days and the patient be kept quiet. He left the room dazed and tired, wondering what the outcome would be.

On the evening of the fourth day he went for the second dressing. As he uncovered the eye, he asked, "Do you see anything?"

"Yes, I do!"

Just then the Sultan's tall and attractive daughter entered the room quietly. As she walked toward the light, the doctor said, "If you see, who is that?"

"That is Firuzeh."

All three were deeply moved, especially Firuzeh, who exclaimed, "My darling father, after four years at last you see me!" She wept for joy.

The doctor at once closed the eye, and with a heart full of gratitude recited his own translation of the hymn,

> *How good is the God we adore,*
> *Our faithful, unchangeable Friend,*
> *Whose love is as great as his power,*
> *And knows neither measure nor end!*
>
> *'Tis Jesus, the First and the Last,*
> *Whose Spirit shall guide us safe home;*
> *We'll praise him for all that is past,*
> *And trust him for all that's to come.*[3]

---

[3]Joseph Hart, 1750

The Sultan was deeply moved by the words and asked that they be repeated for a learned mullah who had entered at that moment. He too was impressed: "It is obvious that among all nations God has some that both know and love him. These words are very effective." The mullah wanted the doctor to operate on his wife's eyes. Sa'eed did so and the operation was so successful on one eye that when he wanted to do the same for the other, she said to him, "I see so well with one eye that I don't want to give you and myself further trouble."

At this time a letter came from Sheikh Ala-ed-Din inviting the doctor to a small village, not his own, for a quiet night's discussion, as he said, "to explain your difficulties and expel your doubts." Sa'eed replied:

"I fear you are making a mistake, for I have no doubts. On the contrary, I am certain. But if Ali, who was the Prophet's son-in-law and for his piety called 'The Lord of Believers,' had no more assurance than was revealed in his cry of anguish, 'Would to God I knew whether I was created for eternal damnation or for bliss!' — if he, who according to Islamic belief had no equal in holiness, makes such an avowal, then what claim is left to you, who are but one among millions of Moslems? How can you, who are constantly a prey to doubts and fears, guide me, who am certain?" He closed by inviting the sheikh to accept Christianity, which leads to perfect assurance.

He gave the letter to Jalal-ed-Din to transmit. The sayyid asked permission to read it. Having done so, he said, "This is your death warrant."

"I cannot leave the sheikh's challenge unanswered," replied Sa'eed. "The day I gave my allegiance to Christ I did not expect to live long, for I had read my death sentence in the Koran. Instead, these thirty years I have lived freely. To die honorably is better than living a coward." On Sa'eed's insistence the letter was sent.

The time had come for the doctor to take his leave. He examined the Sultan's eyes to determine the type of spectacles required and promised to send them without delay. He sent word to the Sultan to disregard the agreement for fifty tomans a day and pay him whatever he considered fair. So on the day of departure the chieftain gave him 200 Turkish gold liras (about $1,000) in addition to the 300 tomans surreptitiously handed to Bagher, a fine mule laden with skins of cooking fat, and a large roll of silk for Rebka.

After farewells the doctor started for Senneh with an armed escort of fifty men, twenty riding, the rest on foot. The road was everywhere covered with snow. Jalal-ed-Din repeatedly asked Sa'eed to change his hat for a turban as less conspicuous, lest it prove an excellent target for some sharpshooter lying in ambush.

At one place they turned off from the direct route, the reason being given that the road chosen was better in winter. Sentinels from the escort were stationed at high points along the way, and at one village they were joined by a further guard. Sa'eed wondered at the necessity for so much precaution, but after arrival at Senneh, Jalal-ed-Din gave the explanation. When Sheikh Ala-ed-Din received the doctor's letter, he and another influential ecclesiastic were so infuriated that they sent a well-known brigand, Mahmud Khan by name, with his robber band to intercept Sa'eed and put him to death. When the Sultan learned of this, he dispatched his fastest courier to catch Jalal-ed-Din with the message: "Do not go by Ariz, I beseech you. At my old age do not drag my hands into bloodshed, for I swear that if a hair of the doctor's head is touched, I will burn the entire countryside, and I will cause such bloodshed that it will become a byword to future generations."

When the Sultan's escort reached one village, to Sa'eed's horror they fell to looting the inhabitants. Bleating sheep and goats were dragged out of their sheds and slaughtered before the eyes of their owners. Frightened chickens were chased and killed. Even the villagers were driven out from under their warm *kursis* to provide a night's lodging for these rough men. Sa'eed leaned help-

lessly against a wall, watching this cruel lawlessness, re-
flecting with astonishment that he had actually been staying among such people. Later he visited a number of these
plundered victims, trying to make amends for their
losses. "This sort of thing is not really serious," the villagers assured him. "These are rare occasions with the
Sultan's men. At their worst we prefer them to the
tyrants of Senneh!"

At last the doctor reached Senneh, to be congratulated
on every hand on his safe arrival. All sorts of reports
had come in during his absence of the dire things that had
happened to him in Awraman. According to one version
the Sultan's eyes had been ruined and the people had
imprisoned Sa'eed. Other rumors narrated in detail the
miraculous cures he had effected. Letters from Hamadan
showed anxiety on the part of his family and friends. To
allay their fears he telegraphed them word of his safe
arrival in Senneh. For the first time in ten weeks he
enjoyed the luxury of a bed with clean sheets and free
from fleas!

Sa'eed spent a few days in Senneh as the guest of the
Governor. During this time he happened to mention to
one of his friends in the course of conversation that the
one disappointment of his trip was the failure to find the
parchments he had been trying for four years to trace.
To his amazement he found that this friend had received
them as a present from the Salar-ud-Dowleh in return
for a special service rendered him. Great was Sa'eed's
joy when his friend passed them on to him as a gift.

When the day of departure came, Sayyid Jalal-ed-Din
sought out the doctor privately. He looked sad and his
silence betrayed embarrassment. Perceiving this, Dr.
Sa'eed said, "Come in. I was just thinking about you."

"About me? In what connection?"

"O, I was thinking I would miss you."

Tears came into the sayyid's eyes as he said: "You have
taken the words right out of my mouth. All the while
we have been on this trip I have been thinking of the

time I should return to my home village. Now that the
time has come, I am sad at the prospect. You have made
me see the light, and for the help you have been to me
I pray God to bless you always." With mutual regret
they said farewell and parted.

It was already a few days past the middle of December
when Dr. Sa'eed set out for Hamadan with a
double escort as far as Khosrovabad. The countryside
was white with a deep snow. At Khosrovabad the escort
was reduced to four riders. On the third day the chief
of the guard was sure that at a certain point in a valley
robbers would pounce down on them from the hills. He
was right in his surmise, for at that spot three mounted
horsemen appeared on the crest of a hill. The headman
of the escort ordered the caravan to proceed with all
speed while he and his companions prepared to fight.
Isolated from his riders and run down from weeks and
weeks of incessant riding and treating patients, Sa'eed was
seized with a fright of which he was later ashamed. The
bandits circled nearer, but when they saw that the guard
was prepared to shoot if they came closer, they pretended
they were simply coming down into the valley to cross to
the other side. They turned up a hill and disappeared.

It lacked but a day to Christmas when the party
reached Hamadan in safety. What a time of joy was the
reunion with family and friends after an absence of three
long months! The simple comforts of his home seemed
to Sa'eed like royal luxuries after the hardships of his
journey. In deep gratitude he poured out his soul in
thanksgiving to God, as he recalled all the deliverances
from dangers and foes that plotted his death, the successful outcome of his ministry of healing made possible only
by divine help, and the many opportunities to witness to
his faith before the Moslems of his own homeland.

CHAPTER ELEVEN

Doctors Ancient and Modern

Iran's most famous physician lived ten centuries ago. He was Abu Ali ibn Sina, shortened to Abu Sina and anglicized to Avicenna. He was born near Bokhara, now in Russian Turkestan, about A.D. 980. At the age of ten he was well acquainted with the Koran and Arabic classics. He then took up the study of logic, mathematics, astronomy, natural sciences, metaphysics, and medicine in turn. The works available for this last subject were translations of the Greek physicians Hipprocrates and Galen. At the age of seventeen his medical knowledge enabled him to cure the ruler of Bokhara of a critical sickness.

After a period of wandering about Iran he landed in Hamadan, where his cure of the local ruler secured his appointment as prime minister. The army conspired against him (probably on the ground that he was a here-

tic, since he was a philosopher and a physician[1]), looted
his house, and demanded his death. He hid himself for
forty days, when the Amir was again taken sick and
again cured by Avicenna, who was reinstated to his former position of authority. After the Amir's death he
went to Isfahan, where he remained until near the close
of his life. Accompanying the ruler of Isfahan on an
expedition against Hamadan, he was taken seriously ill on
the road and died (1037). He was buried in Hamadan.[2]

Avicenna was an intellectual prodigy with an amazing
memory. He wrote over a hundred books or brochures
of varying length covering "logic, metaphysics, theology,
psychology, mysticism, medicine, chemistry, alchemy,
botany, zoology, mathematics, and music."[3] He also wrote
poetry. Long before the days of modern medicine he
achieved a great reputation as a physician. His medical
writings, translated into Latin, dominated the western
world for a period of five centuries and his name is a
landmark in the history of medicine. It was these
medical treatises that Sa'eed had studied in his early days
of training.[4]

At some time prior to World War I, Sir William Osler,
Regius Professor of Medicine at Oxford and former professor at the University of Pennsylvania and John Hop-
kins, and world-renowned authority in his field, had tried
to secure an Avicenna manuscript in Arabic. He wrote to
Dr. A. R. Neligan, physician to the British Legation in
Teheran, who at once referred Osler's request to Dr.
Sa'eed, his friend of many years. By a strange combina-
tion of circumstances, a short time after receiving this
unusual appeal it was given to Sa'eed to cure a prominent

---

[1]Margoliuth, *Lectures Delivered to the Persia Society* 1913-1914 —
Morrison & Gibb, Ltd.

[2]This brief account of Avicenna's life is taken from *Avicenna:
Scientist and Philosopher*, a Millenary Symposium edited by G. M.
Wickens — Luzac & Co., Ltd., 1952.

[3]H. G. Dwight, *Persian Miniatures*, p. 303 — Doubleday, Page & Co.,
1918.

[4]See page 67.

member of the Sufi[5] group in Hamadan of a difficult case of
a troublesome disease. For two hundred years his family
had held a position of leadership in the community both
in theosophy and the practice of medicine. Their knowledge in the latter field had been derived from Razi[6] and
Avicenna. On the shelves of his patient's library the
doctor had seen an old manuscript copy of Avicenna's
Signs and Warnings,[7] a philosophical work dealing with
logic and physics. This he accepted from his grateful
client in lieu of a fee and sent it to Dr. Osler with the following lines penned on the flyleaf:

> Copied in the year A.H. 761[8] (1360) by one who
> carries back his ancestors to a man who studied directly
> under Avicenna himself in Hamadan, the last home of
> the great philosopher. Presented to Sir William Osler, to
> whose sound teachings the profession all the world over
> owes so much, by M. Sa'eed, July 1913.

This incident marked the commencement of a correspondence between the two men that deepened into a lifelong friendship. Sir William gratefully acknowledged
the safe receipt of the manuscript and expressed an eager
desire for the complete works of the great philosopher
and physician, including his poems. It soon became
evident that Osler's enthusiasm for Avicenna extended
beyond the limited horizon of a book lover: it resulted
from a great admiration for the celebrated doctor of the
Middle Ages. He held the writings of the famous Persian
in such esteem that he launched a serious proposal for
the restoration of his tomb.

This tomb was a small, dirty, brick structure, located
just off one of the side streets of Hamadan. Sir William
asked for a description of the building with photographs.
Sa'eed described its pitiful state of dilapidation with de-
teriorating dome and the inside "black with the smoke of
wood, opium, and hashish used by the dervishes who take

---

[5]Sufis are Mohammedan mystics.
[6]See footnote page 67.
[7]The Arabic name is *Al Isharat val Tanbihat.*
[8]A. H. is the abbreviation for *Anno Hegirae*, i.e. in the year of the
Hegira.

shelter there." This graphic account constituted a strong
appeal to Sir William in his plan for restoration.

During the following months Dr. Sa'eed began to contemplate a third trip to Europe. His older son, Samuel,
had been away in England for eleven years except for a
brief visit to Iran in 1911 and was now taking higher
studies in engineering. The younger son, Lemuel, had
been there about seven years and still had another year
to complete his general education. The urge to see them
was compelling. As for himself, the ceaseless toil of ten
years called for a change. At fifty his hair was nearly
all gray. Ever since his breakdown in Sweden he had
been subject to severe heart pains. Extreme exhaustion
or high altitudes brought on sharp attacks.

The serious condition of a patient furnished the occasion needed. A young Assyrian of seventeen from a
family of consequence in Senneh was brought to him for
consultation. After several weeks of careful observation
he came to the conclusion that he was suffering from
schizophrenia. While strongly convinced of the correct-
ness of his diagnosis he hoped he was mistaken. A
proposal to take him to Europe for consultation and
treatment was gladly received by the boy's family.

Upon arriving in Berlin, Dr. Sa'eed took his patient to
the celebrated Dr. Oppenheim for examination. He presented briefly the history of the case, mentioning his investigations and findings. Oppenheim, who had barely
taken notice of Sa'eed at first, his interest being in the
patient, looked up in astonishment. "Who are you? Where
are you from?"

"I am a Kurd. I was brought up in Kurdistan."

"All that aside, where did you study? You speak the
language of experts and specialists."

"I studied in Persia. My teacher was an American
missionary."

"No, no. That will not suffice."

Sa'eed then told him of his studies in England. Oppenheim led the way to another room. Since the patient

knew no English, it was possible to discuss his case freely in his presence. After a thorough examination Dr. Oppenheim concurred in Sa'eed's diagnosis and wrote a letter to an institution suited to the boy's needs. He also included a word of caution in the margin: "Be careful! The physician accompanying him knows a great deal!" Business over, he showed Sa'eed a number of his own publications and courteously accompanied him to the door with good wishes when he left.

His subsequent trip to England gave him an opportunity to visit Professor Edward G. Browne, celebrated Orientalist and Persian scholar at Cambridge University,[9] with whom Sa'eed had had previous acquaintance. He exhibited the precious parchments he had been able to secure in Kurdistan and related the singular story of their discovery in the mountains of Awraman. He left them with Prof. Browne for further examination. They were bilingual, written in Greek and Pahlevi characters, dating from 80 B.C., and they awakened a wide interest among the paleographists of Europe. Due to a misunderstanding Prof. Browne turned them over to Cambridge University as a gift, but later through a disinterested friend he learned of his mistake and arranged for their return, greatly to Dr. Sa'eed's embarrassment. Eventually the matter was cleared up in good taste and a new friendship resulted from the incident.

Following this, Dr. Sa'eed made a call on Sir William Osler to convey to him a rare manuscript in Arabic, Avicenna's masterpiece, *Canon of Medicine*,[10] a voluminous treatise setting forth the principles and practice of medicine, the purchase of which had been arranged by the Bodleian Library.[11] In addition to this he brought photographs of Avicenna's tomb, which Dr. Osler had been desirous of securing.

---

[9]Prof. Browne had a special interest in Persia, having spent a year there. He was the author of a four-volume *Literary History of Persia*.

[10]The Arabic name is *Kitab ul Qanun fil Tibb*.

[11]The Bodleian Library at Oxford has one of the finest collections of Oriental manuscripts in all Europe.

The meeting of the two doctors is picturesquely described by Dr. Harvey Cushing, eminent American brain
surgeon, in his *Life of Sir William Osler* in these words:

> Among other pilgrims to 13 Norham Gardens who ap-
> peared at this time was a foreign-looking physician, Dr.
> M. Sa'eed, who bore under his arm an illuminated manu-
> script of the Canon of Avicenna, wrapped in a shawl
> almost as old, together with two other books without
> which, he said, he never moved—his Bible and Osler's
> *Practice of Medicine.*[12]

At first Sir William, who had had a mental picture of
an Oriental practitioner, was reluctant to call Sa'eed
"doctor," but he was soon impressed with his knowledge
and personality.   After a short acquaintance he gladly
invited him to the sessions of the Royal Society of Medicine and introduced him as "Dr. Sa'eed of Persia" to the
famous professors and physicians at Oxford.   Many
interesting hours were spent together in examination of
rare manuscripts at the Bodleian Library.   Osler's regard
for Sa'eed grew into genuine admiration.   He also came
from a pious family.   He was a student of the Bible and
it seems at one time had contemplated medical missionary
service.   For Sa'eed's work he had heartfelt sympathy
and admiration.   A short while afterward he presented
Sa'eed with an autographed picture of himself together
with the latest edition of his *Practice of Medicine.*

A picture of Avicenna's tomb reproduced from one of Dr.
Sa'eed's photographs was at once published through Dr.
Osler's agency in medical journals and other periodicals
to reinforce an appeal made by him to members of his
profession all over the world to raise the funds necessary
for the project he had in mind.   "It is a pity," he was
saying with feeling, "that the tomb of such a great
philosopher is allowed to remain in this ruined state.   We
must raise funds and build a beautiful memorial over the
grave."   He also had Sa'eed speak before the historical
section of the Royal Society of Medicine.

---

[12]Vol. II, page 376 — Oxford University Press.

Sir Willliam's enthusiasm, while admirable in its motives, was unfortunately not combined with a knowledge of Eastern ways. Sa'eed cautioned him that the mere construction of a building would not suffice, for in time it would assuredly become the haunt of dervishes, who would cause Avicenna further headache from the smoke of their opium and hashish! He suggested that part of the money raised be put in some bank and its interest used for the maintenance of the property and to provide a small salary for a keeper, who would be responsible for its care. The suggestion met with Osler's immediate approval. So Dr. Sa'eed at once wrote to Dr. Funk of the American Mission in Hamadan for estimates and solicited the aid of the British Minister in Teheran to secure necessary authorization for the project.

In the meantime Sa'eed benefitted from his stay in London by taking advanced medical work both at the London Polyclinic, where he had studied before, and at the Central Ophthalmic Hospital, where his former teachers were extremely pleased with his knowledge and skill and spared no trouble in acquainting him with the latest methods in ophthalmology. Samuel was also finishing his engineering course and it was his father's great pleasure to attend his graduation exercises and see him win prizes for the best papers on two different subjects.[13] Professor Browne was so delighted that a Persian had won these high honors that he sent Samuel his personal congratulations and a set of his four-volume *Literary History of Persia*.

When Dr. Sa'eed was planning to return to Persia, Dr. Osler renewed the subject of Avicenna's tomb and charged him with the responsibility of approaching the proper authorities. After his arrival in his homeland he wrote to the Regent in an attempt to get the young king, Ahmad Shah, to accept honorary sponsorship of the committee on the project, among whose personnel would

---

[13]On *Sewage and Sewage Disposal* and *Oxygen-Acetylene Welding*.

appear the names of celebrities from England, France, and Persia. His efforts, however, had hardly borne fruit when the sudden outbreak of World War I cut short all plans for a commemorative undertaking of this nature.

Although Persia declared her neutrality in the war, the country was occupied by contending armies. In the summer of 1916 a Turkish contingent came up from Baghdad and occupied Hamadan. With their approach Dr. Sa'eed with his daughter Sarah and her family and Lemuel left for Teheran. In fact almost all of the Christian community, with the exception of the Jewish converts and the American missionaries, whose country was still neutral, fled the city. Characteristically, Rebka refused to leave. Lemuel left Teheran to join her and reached Hamadan only a few hours before the Turkish army.

During their occupation of Hamadan the Turks, disappointed in their efforts to lay their hands on the "apostate," wreaked their vengeance on Sa'eed's country place, where they cut down thousands of dollars worth of trees. The only explanation given was that he had treated Russian soldiers in their occupation of the city during the previous months and that his son was reported to be serving with the British army in France. Word of this reached the British government and Dr. Sa'eed was offered 700 pounds as indemnity. In his letter to the British Minister declining the offer, he quoted the words of Jacob to Esau: ". . . Because God hath dealt graciously with me, and because I have enough";[14] adding, "I do not wish my children to do good in the expectation of a reward."

Later in the war, when British forces were occupying Hamadan, occurred the pathetic flight of the Assyrian nation from their home in the Urumia plain and over the Turkish border, a flight in which this people was decimated by the sword, disease, and starvation. Dr. Sa'eed's large house of twelve rooms, many cellars, and three

---

[14]Gen. 33:11

Mausoleum of Avicenna in Hamadan

yards was put at the disposal of refugees who remained in Hamadan. In Teheran also he opened his home and purse freely to them and sought to help where help was needed. Some thought that in this he was receiving funds from abroad, but actually not a penny came from outside. Among those he had the privilege of helping was the family of Kasha Yohanan, to whom he owed so much.

One of the Assyrians whom the doctor was attending remarked to others: "He is a Kurd and many of those who looted and killed our people were Kurds also. Look at the difference!"

"I do it," said Sa'eed, "because an Assyrian was the means of leading me to Christ, and I owe the gospel of salvation to this people. If everyone of you had been worthy of the name you bear and each had tried to lead one soul to Christ, today you would have no enemies."

Meanwhile Sir William Osler wrote that he had lost his son[15] in the war, but even this tragedy did not seem to have dimmed his interest in Avicenna. With unabated zeal he took up the project which had been so rudely interrupted. The correspondence between the two doctors continued. At this time Sa'eed ran across a copy of the medical writings of Razi, the Persian doctor who antedated Avicenna. To Osler he wrote of his discovery: "Just think of it! One thousand years ago Zacharia[16] said the same thing as you concerning pains in the appendix region. He insists that in such cases no purge of any kind is to be administered to the patient!"

Sir William replied enthusiastically: "How extraordinary! So Zacharia actually knew this fact a thousand years ago. The doctors of our own day haven't quite learned this!" He begged that the manuscript be sent to him—a great sacrifice to Sa'eed, for he too was a lover of books. He was sad to part with the newly found treasure; nevertheless, he sent the book to Osler.

---

[15] Lt. Revere Osler of the Royal Artillery, a great-great-grandson of Paul Revere.
[16] Another name for Razi.

Eight days later Sa'eed's bookseller friend dropped in, and lo, among his collection of odd manuscripts the doctor found an older and even better copy of the same book! At once he paid the price demanded and was elated to have it, but only a short time elapsed till this copy went to Dr. Cushing. Cushing was at that time writing Osler's biography and he asked Sa'eed for the correspondence he had had with him. Gradually their friendship grew despite the distance between Persia and America, and continued till the end of Cushing's life. When his biography was finished, he sent a copy to Sa'eed, also an autographed picture of himself.

The story of Osler and Avicenna, however, had to end tragically. Immediately after the war was over, he wrote to Sa'eed again: "Get ready; let us proceed with our plans without further delay." This was the last letter Sir William wrote of Avicenna. He fell ill shortly afterwards and died. This was a big blow to the project for a memorial to the celebrated Persian physician.

With the funds raised, the land around the tomb was fenced in and a building erected, in which there was a reading room in use for some years, but the structure was nothing to do credit to that great sage of the Middle Ages. In 1939 the Iranian Ministry of Education asked several architects, including Samuel, to design a combined library and mausoleum for Avicenna. While the plans were under consideration war again brought foreign armies to neutral Iran and the matter was set aside.

As the thousandth anniversary[17] of Avicenna's birth approached, however, the Iranian government revived the project, determined to celebrate the occasion with a monument that would be truly worthy of the great philosopher-physician. Plans were drawn for an elaborate mausoleum with a high concrete tower above the grave and a library in connection with it. This was erected and in May 1954 the structure was dedicated in the presence of a large group of Iranian celebrities, including the King

[17]Calculated by the Mohammedan calendar.

and Queen, and distinguished Orientalists from abroad.[18]
The avenue in front of the tomb was named in honor of
Avicenna and a statue of him was erected in the circle
at the upper end.

What a privilege it would have been to both Sir William Osler and Dr. Sa'eed, if they could have shared in
this impressive celebration!

---

[18]A recent issue of 10-rial (one toman) bank notes by the National
Bank of Iran has a fine view of this mausoleum and library.

CHAPTER TWELVE

The Physician—The Family— The Man

After World War I conditions in Iran changed rapidly. An army officer rose swiftly to power, becoming Minister of War, then Prime Minister, and finally in February 1926 he was crowned Reza Shah. A commanding personality with a forward look, he introduced sweeping reforms in government, in education, and in society. Roads were built all over the country and made safe from brigandage. A railroad was laid from the Caspian Sea in the north to the Persian Gulf on the southwest. Fine government buildings were erected in the capital. New avenues were cut and paved in provincial cities. Conscription was introduced to build up an army. Vital statistics and titles to property were registered. Factories were built. Many new schools were opened. The University of Teheran was founded. Newspapers and magazines came into being.

The power of the mullahs was greatly curtailed. Women were emancipated from their veiled seclusion of thirteen centuries. These many changes engendered a new pride of country and a fervid spirit of nationalism.

With all of these reforms came greater security. As a result, the life of Dr. Sa'eed, now settled permanently in the capital city, moved along quietly in the busy routine of his practice, gradually slowing down as the sixties passed into the seventies.

His home and clinic were near the center of the city, located on a pleasant avenue lined on both sides by tall plane trees. There were small shops on either side of the property and across the street the offices of the War Department and the compound of the American Presbyterian Mission. There were two gates, one for the clinic with a modest sign over it, and the other for the home. The rooms of the house and the clinic were built around three sides of a courtyard, in the center of which was the customary pool, surrounded by flower beds and laurels, acacia and fir trees.

An early riser, the doctor had his time of private devotions, followed by breakfast, and was in his clinic by half past eight. There he saw a steady stream of patients till noon and from two o'clock till dark, except when he went out into the city for house calls. Usually the waiting rooms were full of patients, while part of the dispensary and sometimes even the library were used to take care of the overflow.

At work he wore the customary doctor's white topcoat over his street clothes, his stethoscope hanging conveniently around his neck or bulging out of his side pocket. His rather portly bearing, dignified language and manner, with an unmistakable air of authority, created a feeling of respect and confidence in those who sought his treatment. In examining his patients he was thorough without being needlessly lengthy. He never took down case histories: his keen intellect and retentive memory took the place of written records. With directness and precision and without much laboratory support he would arrive at the right conclusions, for he seemed to possess an unusual accuracy in diagnosis. One thing alone used to irritate him, and that was disobedience to his orders. Always dependent upon God for help and guidance, he carried the needs of his patients to the Great Physician in simple trust and interceded for them.

In addition to his daily ministry of healing and individual conversations with patients, Dr. Sa'eed continued his Bible readings twice a week. On Sundays the gatherings, held in the large dining room, were especially for Christians, while on Thursdays Moslems and other interested individuals came. A certain book of the Bible would be selected for systematic study. Nothing was prepared beforehand: the doctor spoke out of his vast acquaintance with the Word of God that was the result of years of study and led those present into the depths and heights of its teachings.

In spite of his busy life he was not mechanical in the strict observance of fixed hours. He always seemed to have time for everything. He was never too weary to respond to a call for help. Sometimes of an afternoon he would walk for miles, visiting the sick or the indigent, bringing them words of cheer. Bible in hand, he would read and pray with them, often inviting them to send some one to his house for needed medicines or clothing.

The home was characterized by hospitality. Though not given to entertainment, it was constantly open to anyone who happened to drop in. There was always enough on the table to provide for the casual visitor. Friends coming to Teheran were sometimes guests for weeks. There was an atmosphere of informal cordiality to welcome them. Among the most frequent callers were members of the missionary group.

Rebka was indisputably the mistress of the household. Thoroughly efficient, she ran everything smoothly and competently. Through capable training she made excellent servants or cooks out of the raw material she em-

ployed. Money matters were largely in her hands; with
a twinkle in his eye the doctor would say, "Rebka is the
purse holder in this house." He was so artless in business
matters that without her shrewd and able management
he might well have been grossly imposed upon because
of his own generosity and others' willingness to accept
help.

While Rebka was capable in handling money, she was
by no means stingy. Like her husband she was extremely
generous, especially toward the poor of her people and
the refugees. On many occasions, when in a hired carriage, she would ask the driver to stop, so that she might
help some poor lad on the street whom she recognized as
an Assyrian. The underfed and destitute of her people,
the stranger and the lonely soldier from afar received her
aid unasked. Many were the blessings called down upon
her by these grateful strangers.

Added to her generosity was her salty wit. Directed
toward those of her family circle, it did much to build up
the charm of the home life.

Of the three children, Sarah was living with her husband and family in Hamadan. Samuel, after completing
his studies in England, had volunteered for British army
service and was severely wounded while on active duty
on the Continent. Later he was sent to Persia as an
officer of the Royal Engineers. After the war he became
architect for the Imperial Bank of Iran, a British organization. He was in charge of their extensive properties all
over Iran and Iraq and responsible for the planning and
construction of their new buildings. He eventually
married an American missionary, a short-term teacher
from Wells College. After nineteen years of service with
the bank he resigned and in 1942 rejoined his family in
Mexico, New York.

The younger son, Lemuel, returned to England after
World War I and was employed by some publishers as an
illustrating artist. After several years he came down
with a serious spinal disease and was forced to enter a

London hospital. When word of his critical condition reached his father, he kept the situation a secret from the family so as to spare them anxiety, but it was a heavy burden for him. After Lemuel's condition became hopeless, he broke the news to the others. Lemuel died in February 1927 at the age of thirty-one and was buried in London. It was a bitter blow to the bereaved parents.

No account of the family would be complete without further reference to Kaka. Perhaps no experience in the whole span of Dr. Sa'eed's Christian life constituted a stronger testimony to the truth and power of Christianity than the change it wrought in his brother. It took several years of careful study and thought after Kaka's first visit to Hamadan before he was ready to accept the Christian faith heart and soul. But once he took the final step there was no turning back. To see the proud mullah of Kurdistan serving as a hostler to support himself made one think of Him who "made himself of no reputation, and took upon him the form of a servant."[1] From this menial job he rose to have charge of the American Mission boys' boarding school, and then became an evangelist. For long years he was busy distributing tracts and leaflets, talking with men in the bazaars of Hamadan, or traveling on a donkey from town to town in the surrounding country, reading and interpreting the Bible to anyone who would listen — sometimes in a teahouse where idlers gathered, sometimes under the *kursi* of a peasant's home, sometimes squatting in the dust of a village street where a group of men had gathered to pass the time of day. This work was his glory and his joy. When weak in his old age and severely handicapped by deafness, he still asked to be allowed to make these trips and continue the work to which he had given his life.

In the summer of 1935 the two brothers were visiting together at the Mission garden outside of Hamadan toward the mountains. Kaka was well on toward eighty and Sa'eed seventy-two. Seated in the shade of a giant

---

[1]Phil. 2:7

Kaka

walnut tree, they were reviewing the experiences of rich, full lives. Their thoughts turned back to their past in the city of their birth.

"Kaka," said Sa'eed, "I'm not unwilling to see Senneh once again."

"What about me?" retorted Kaka. "I haven't seen it for fifty-one years."

The very next day came an urgent telephone call for the doctor to go to Senneh to see the wife of the Vakil-ul-Molk. He declined, for he knew it would be a matter of seeing not just one patient, but scores, and he did not feel equal to it. Finally he consented, provided his son-in-law, Dr. Tatevos, would go along to help him. This arrangement agreed to, Sa'eed sent word to Kaka: "Get ready! We are going to Kurdistan! You were wanting to go. Now, not only are you invited, but they are begging you to go!" And so they went together.

Imagine Kaka's feelings on returning to the city of his youth after half a century! Both brothers were royally received. While Sa'eed was busy seeing patients, Kaka was invited out day and night. He made a complete tour of the city, visiting his parents' graves, the ruin of the old homestead, and numerous mosques he had frequented as a Moslem. He spoke freely everywhere and distributed tracts. The visit lasted eight days.

On the ninth day, when they were leaving, a number of the nobility gathered at the Governor's residence to see them off. In order to make Kaka talk, one of the men teased him by saying in the presence of the others: "Why do you want to go back to Hamadan? Stay with us and return to your faith. We will give you a good wife and all the money you wish."

"I possess the gift of eternal life," Kaka replied. "What do I care for money and the goods of this world? If you would fill this huge palace with gold sovereigns, even that would not tempt me."

"Why, then, were you so determined on the persecution of your brother, going from street to street with a gun in your hand, seeking to kill him?"

"That was through ignorance, just as you today, ignorant of the gift of eternal life in Christ, think to persuade me with money to return to Islam."

Such was Kaka's parting testimony to the people of his native city, where he had once sought his brother's life for the same witness. He never saw Senneh again. In the fall of that year he was suddenly laid low with a stroke of paralysis that rendered him helpless. After some months he made an amazing recovery. He wrote to Sa'eed as follows:

"While I was at the hospital one night, I had a heart-to-heart talk with the Lord. I said to him, 'Master, with joy I am looking forward to being with thyself, which is far better; but if thy will for me is still to remain, then graciously give me strength to attend to my daily work of passing out tracts to people on the street until thou art ready to call me home.' Now I spend two hours each day giving out tracts and pamphlets. I am deeply glad of this opportunity."

Now past eighty and no longer able to hold conversations because of his extreme deafness, this aged soldier of the Cross walked from street to street handing out leaflets. On one of his usual excursions he was knocked down by a carriage and run over. For ten months he was bedridden, tenderly cared for by his son, a physician. In March 1940 he died at the age of eighty-four, steadfast to the end in the faith he had sought so zealously to propagate.

Turning to Dr. Sa'eed himself, one finds it hard to know which of his many fine traits of character to emphasize. Perhaps four may be selected.

First of all, he was a man of *rugged independence. It* goes without saying that no one could have made such an earnest search for truth as he did without this quality. He was altogether unwilling to accept ready-made beliefs handed down from others. Everything had to be investigated and tested at first hand. When he first came in contact with Christianity, he felt he must make a thorough study of the Bible, comparing its teachings with those of the Koran. He learned Hebrew so that he might assure himself that there had been no corruption of the Old Testament in translation. How could he have maintained his Christian faith through all the years of persecution without such a spirit of independence?

In the choice of a wife he overstepped the bounds of custom and tradition by marrying a girl of another race.

He was not content to be under obligation to the Mission for his means of support, but was determined to seek a profession whereby he would be responsible to no one: so it was that he studied to become a physician. It was this same trait that made him dissatisfied with organized Christianity as he found it and led him to seek out a group in which each member regarded himself as a priest in direct communication with God and dependent on no minister or church. To the end of his life, though on the friendliest terms with the Protestant Christians and ready to preach in their services when invited or to review their tracts and books before publication, he yet held aloof from membership in their organizations or service through them.

Dr. Sa'eed was *deeply spiritual.* It was the hope of finding fuller satisfaction for his spiritual aspirations that led him, while still a Moslem, to turn in discontent with orthodox Islam to the Naqshbandis. And when he became a Christian it was this same urge, as we have seen, that constituted one of the reasons for his trip to Sweden. Throughout his whole career spiritual considerations were the dominating factor in his life.

From the time when in Senneh he began a serious study of the Bible, to his last days the Word of God was his constant companion and the source of his inspiration. A glance at the pages of his well-worn Bible with margins marked and remarked would suffice to show how faithfully he pored over it. No day opened without its perusal; in the noon hour of rest he would refer to it; and at the day's close it brought him peace for the night. When he stepped abroad he had it with him, to be ready to read to patient or friend. In perplexity it was his guide, in distress his comfort. His memory was richly stored with its treasures.

Along with Bible study went prayer, which was as vital to him as the air he breathed. Even as a Moslem he was dissatisfied to have his prayers a mere repetition of words said by rote. How he pitied those poor Mohammedans who said their stated prayers ignorant of the meaning of the Arabic words they pronounced! Again and again the guidance that he needed came to him when he was on his knees, perhaps changing some decision he had already made. And his prayers were made in faith. When word came to him in Teheran that his little grandson in Hamadan was seriously ill, his recovery was of course a subject of prayer at family worship. Day by day for a week the news became more alarming. On the night when the news was darkest he prayed: "Our precious Lord Jesus, we thank thee humbly for having heard our prayers and granted our request on behalf of our dear Willie." The next message from Hamadan brought the good news that the grandson was on the road to recovery.

The presence of God was very real to him. He felt a deep sense of intimacy with his Heavenly Father and fellowship with him. On return from his dangerous trip to Senneh and Awraman, in the fervor of his prayer of gratitude for deliverance from perils and for the successful outcome of his work of healing, the presence of Christ was so real to him that he threw himself at his feet to kiss them. Perhaps his most loved hymn, certainly one that he often quoted, contained this stanza:

> *I have seen the Face of Jesus —*
> *Tell me not of aught beside;*
> *I have heard the Voice of Jesus—*
> *All my heart is satisfied.*[2]

No one who knew Dr. Sa'eed intimately could fail to be impressed with his intense and bold *evangelistic spirit*. The faith that he had struggled so hard to win was not a prize to be enjoyed by himself alone, but a gift to be shared. Many have been the secret converts from Islam, convinced of the truth of Christianity and ready in private to acknowledge Christ as their Savior, but fearful of the personal consequences if they should make open confession. On the contrary, not only was Dr. Sa'eed

---

[2]"Beyond the Brightness of the Sun," by Mrs. Frances Bevan.

courageous to make known his faith, but he sought every opportunity to lead others to its acceptance. We have seen how in the early days in Senneh he was not content to hide his light under a bushel, but felt that he must share it with his boyhood friends and found joy in so doing. "Only then," he recalled later, "did I realize how much I had lost by not witnessing to Christ earlier."

His medical practice was a means for evangelism. He was not satisfied to meet only the physical ailments of his patients, but he sought to minister to their spiritual needs as well. In their homes he would read to them from the Bible, talk with them, pray with them. On his journeys he would speak of his religion to the people in whose homes he stayed. When summoned before the authorities he did not hesitate to witness to his faith. He testified to landowners and army officers, to mullahs and governors, to sayyids and tribal chieftains. He wrote the whole story of the Gospels in Kurdish poetry, a labor of love spread over thirty-five years, that he might reach his own people.

Much of the persecution that befell him was due to his constant talking about his religion. Had he been content to practise medicine and make no effort to reach the spiritual wants of his patients, he would have avoided much of his trouble. It was for this reason that the Governor of Hamadan once said to him: "Why do you go and speak about religious matters and stir up the mullahs? Go and keep quiet." But Dr. Sa'eed was one of those who felt that he must obey God rather than men. Like the apostles of old, he could not but speak the things he had seen and heard. And since his testimony came from his own personal experience, it was telling and effective.

A fourth trait that characterized Dr. Sa'eed was his *generous treatment of his enemies.* Whenever opportunity came to serve one who had persecuted him or sought his life, he was more than ready to seize it. If anyone kept Christ's precepts to "love your enemies, do

good to them which hate you,"[3] it was he. Instances of
this might be multiplied; two must suffice.

One Thursday afternoon while he was conducting a
Bible reading in his home, a man in the uniform of an
army captain entered the room, evidently in great dis-
comfort from an abscess on his neck. Dr. Sa'eed greeted
him cordially and asked him if he minded waiting till
the Bible reading was over. The man willingly sat down.
When the doctor had finished, he stepped to his dispensary to sterilize a scalpel. After a moment of silence the
captain addressed the group: "You gentlemen don't know
me. Long years ago I sought to kill this man, but this is
the way he has treated me and my relatives all these
years." After the minor operation was over, he took a
cup of tea and left. The others looked to the doctor for
an explanation.

"The man you have just seen," said he, "is Mahmud
Khan, formerly the notorious bandit of Kurdistan! On
my way back from Awraman this man was sent out by
Sheikh Ala-ed-Din with a band of his henchmen to intercept our caravan in the mountains and kill me, but God's
mercy preserved us by a change of route."[4] For a year
and a half Mahmud Khan and twenty-five members of
his family were confined in a house in Teheran. During
this time the doctor had served as their physician without
charge.

The Imam Jum'eh of Hamadan was another notable
example of Dr. Sa'eed's turning the other cheek. It was
due to this man's instrumentality that the doctor suffered
the bitter persecution of 1904 in Hamadan which led to
the breaking up of his home and practice there and necessitated his escape to Teheran.[5] When in the summer
of 1911 he returned to Hamadan for a period of rest the
Imam Jum'eh, very ill from a stomach ulcer, sent for
him. The doctor nursed him back to health. Each year

[3]Luke 6:27
[4]See page 147.
[5]See pp. 103ff.

*Pages from Dr. Sa'eed's Bible (open at the
First Chapter of Ephesians)*

when Dr. Sa'eed returned to Hamadan for the summer, the Imam Jum'eh called on him and he returned the call. Both the man and his household were always given free medical aid. When he finally moved to Teheran the same course was pursued. The first time he called on the doctor in the capital, a mullah friend was with him. To this friend he said: "I am ashamed before the doctor, for I have done him a great deal of evil, which he has returned only by kindness. On one occasion he even saved my life."

Later on this same man, calling on a Christian physician from Hamadan, remarked that he had been to see Dr. Sa'eed, adding: "I am astonished. I have done everything I could to end his life, yet he always shows me kindness."

The physician replied: "He is only a Kurd, but you must consider the cause of the difference between him and the other members of his race. It is the power of the person of Christ."

It was indeed "the power of the person of Christ" that made Dr. Sa'eed the noble man that he was, that changed the proud, fanatical Kurd into the humble, self-giving Christian. It was because of this transformation and the great service that he rendered to his fellow men that Sir Mortimer Durand, for some years British Minister in Teheran, volunteered this indirect testimony to him: "If in all the years of its activities the American Mission had achieved nothing more than the conversion of Dr. Sa'eed, then its labors had been amply repaid."

CHAPTER THIRTEEN

The Last Years

It was the summer of 1937. Dr. Sa'eed had gone to Hamadan as usual for his annual rest from the strain of active life in Teheran. Under the shade of the willow trees bordering the terrace in their country garden the family was enjoying their afternoon tea around the simmering samovar. The rhythmic play of the fountain in the little pool near by and the scent of roses perfuming the air added their contribution to the idyllic scene. On the doctor's knee his youngest grandchild was telling him of her latest adventure in the woods gathering wild flowers.

"Look, grandfather!" she said, pointing to the shaded walk leading to the terrace. Two men were approaching. Even in this retreat the doctor could not completely escape from those who sought him out for medical advice. Unannounced visitors frequently dropped in for a friendly call. As the men drew near, one was seen to be in the uniform of a police officer, the other in civilian clothes. The strangers were courteously received.

After being served with tea, the officer said: "I bring you greetings from the Chief of Police. He is very sorry to inconvenience you, Doctor, but he has a patient and has sent his own car to take you to the city."

"How long has the patient been ill? Is it a man or a woman?"

"About two weeks. He is a man."

Dr. Sa'eed hurriedly picked up his physician's bag and accompanied the men without delay. Not until a policeman sat on each side of him in the car did he realize that he was under arrest. The entrance from the garden being at some distance from the terrace, the family saw nothing of the car, but one of Sa'eed's nephews, returning to the garden, saw him pass and sensed the situation.

Meanwhile the doctor was cudgeling his brain to find some clue for his apprehension, but he could think of nothing. The officer remained silent to let him recover from the shock. After a while he laid his hand on Sa'eed's knee and said: "It must all be a mistake. You will simply have to answer a few questions."

"Do you know why I am wanted?"

"Why, it is nothing serious. I understand it is in connection with a letter you wrote recently." Those were the days of dictatorship when the mails were carefully censored to detect any insubordination or criticism of the government.

Suddenly it dawned on the doctor. Six days before he had written a letter of condolence to the daughter of a Kurdish chief who had recently died in Teheran at the age of eighty. In the process of bringing various disaffected tribes under control, Reza Shah had found it necessary to hold some of their leaders as hostages. This particular man had been allowed full liberty within the limits of Teheran, but his movements had been carefully watched. Sa'eed had been his physician during his long illness and a strong bond of friendship had been forged between them as a result of many heart-to-heart spiritual talks. The doctor could not conceive how anything in his letter of condolence could by the wildest stretch of the imagination be interpreted to have political significance.

At police headquarters the interrogating officer produced a letter out of his desk drawer and bluntly asked Sa'eed if he recognized the writing. "It is mine," he replied.

"In that case you have some explanations to make," was the stern reply. "This is what you wrote to the daughter of the deceased:

" 'Although your father was under government supervision and his every move watched, you must still be glad that he died in his own home, surrounded by his family — not like Sowlat-ud-Dowleh,[1] Taimurtash,[2] and others, some of whom were taken through the country and died in prison.' "

With a dramatic flourish he put the letter down. "Who are you to say that Sowlat-ud-Dowleh and Taimurtash died in prison?"

Sa'eed remained silent. He did not care to tell his examiner that he had been the Sowlat's physician to the end. Besides, the fate of the two men mentioned was a matter of public knowledge.

"You must have been very closely connected with them," the officer continued, "to know so much. How do you know they died, anyway?"

"Politics and political figures do not interest me," replied Dr. Sa'eed. "Only in so far as men's bodies and souls are concerned do I have anything to do with them. If I have unknowingly made a statement contrary to fact, I am sorry, and I shall be obliged if you will enlighten me."

---

[1]Sowlat-ud-Dowleh was the title of the Ilkhani of Chapter 8.

[2]Taimurtash was Minister of the Court during part of Reza Shah's reign.

"Wise men know how to mind their own business,"
the officer snapped back. "That will do for today." He
rang the bell on his desk. A policeman entered. "Show
this gentleman his room."

Eight or nine stone steps led to the room to which he
was conducted. It had an earthen floor covered in part
by a small reed mat. At one end was a wooden bedstead
with scant and questionable bedclothes. He stepped to
the window to look out. Facing him was the tomb of
Avicenna! A flood of memories passed through his mind,
bringing cheer to his heart. Once alone in the privacy
of his room he began to pray for guidance. He was confident that soon everything would be straightened out.
He stretched himself on the hard board bed, covering
his shoulders with his coat. During many years of
travel he had learned to rough it, but at seventy-four,
especially as he was now never completely well, it was
not easy to adjust himself to the wooden bunk and the
torture of mosquitoes. He had little sleep that night.

The next day his son-in-law, Dr. Tatevos, was allowed
to see him and to bring a camp cot and food from home.
He was even allowed to spend the nights with him until
Sa'eed insisted that this was not necessary. On the whole
the police treated him kindly and allowed family and
friends to call, at first with a policeman present but later
without.

Time dragged on without any definite action being
taken and days passed into weeks. It was obvious that
the authorities in Hamadan were awaiting instructions
from the capital. Family and friends worked and prayed
for his release, but the police of Hamadan were power-
less to make any major decision.

News of his imprisonment meanwhile spread far and
wide with a swiftness proportionate to his reputation
and the place he held in many hearts. He was greatly
cheered by many letters of sympathy. One of the most
touching evidences of affection came from the Kurds,
who had once been so bitter in their hostility. Even

though they knew the danger of sympathizing too openly with one in disfavor with the authorities, they did not fail to let him and the public know that in his hour of trial they took his troubles to heart. Some of the highest people in Kurdistan, including a number of the most influential religious leaders, wrote him in words such as these:

"Our constant prayers cover you from head to foot, and we trust the God whom you worship in spirit and in truth will deliver you and bring your innocence to light, leading to your speedy release."

Later Sa'eed wrote exultantly: "Just think of it! A generation ago they were seeking to destroy my life, but now their leaders are praying for my safety!"

After two and a half months he was transferred to Teheran under guard. Many friends were still working for his release. His son Samuel, who knew many influential men through his architectural work for public buildings, had called on various officials high up in the government, but to no avail. He even went to see the Prime Minister, who told him with evident embarrassment that he was under great obligation to his father, for he had cured him when other doctors had proved unable to help him; clearly, he too could do nothing in this matter. He had previously, however, telegraphed Hamadan to extend Dr. Sa'eed all possible privileges and comforts. Dr. Harvey Cushing wrote from America that he had taken the matter up with President Roosevelt. The British and American Legations offered to help, but Samuel asked them to do nothing until he had tried the ultimate authority, Reza Shah himself. The American missionaries had wisely chosen not to interfere, lest their interest react unfavorably, but showed their interest by faithful visiting.

So Samuel wrote a 140-word telegram to the King, briefly reviewing the case, stating that the letter of condolence had been misinterpreted, and asking that his fault, quite unintentional, be forgiven. This was edited

by the Shah's secretary and signed by Rebka. Upon
consultation with the Prime Minister and another member of the Cabinet, they advised postponing its dispatch
for a few days until the horse races at Bandar Shah on
the Caspian Sea, on which occasion His Majesty was always in a good humor. Almost all the Cabinet members
would be present and the secretary would see that the
Prime Minister presented the telegram at the most aus-
picious moment.

This method of approach was evidently effective, for
it was not long until the order was issued for Dr Sa'eed's
release, though even then a guarantee had to be given the
police in writing by someone owning real estate that the
doctor would be produced in person within four hours on
demand, otherwise the guarantor would have to give
himself up and his property be confiscated. They were
not going to take any chances of future trouble with this
traitorous doctor!

It was a great moment when at last Sa'eed arrived
home and rejoined his family. Rejoicing was widespread
when news of his release reached his friends. His imprisonment, without either trial or sentence, had lasted
ninety-nine days. He said it was the best rest he had
had in fifty years!

After his liberation he wrote letters of thanks to the
Prime Minister and others for their interest in his case,
and he received affectionate replies. The Prime Minister's
letter began, "My own very dear Doctor." From all parts
of Iran and from abroad as well, letters of congratulation
poured in. There were many touching messages from
Kurdistan.

The dream to retire from public life and devote his
remaining years to various studies and literary pursuits
seemed about to be realized when in September 1938
Dr. Sa'eed moved to a new house built for him by Samuel.
Here the familiar sign which had hung over his office
entrance for a quarter of a century was no longer in
evidence, but neither this fact nor his advanced age

served to keep away the sick. Every available means was used by persistent patients to find him and receive his help, so that in a short time this anticipated retreat became "open house." "They come," he wrote, "and insist, some of them from far away, and they are very ill. I cannot refuse them, but I get very tired myself." Nevertheless, he was able to devote more time to his studies than in former years.

The doctor set himself to work in the new house with the devotion of a scholar. His letters written at this time retained all the vigor and beauty of his superb penmanship. There was not the least trace of any decline in mental energy. His interests seemed to expand with ongoing years.

The comforts of the new house — all carefully planned and attractively realized through Samuel's capable skill and filial devotion — were greatly appreciated by his aging parents. It was a three-story brick building — a basement and two floors above. The rooms, except those for storage, had the southern exposure so essential in Iran for summer cool and winter warmth. The doctor's quarters covered his various requirements for library, guests and patients. His bedroom was flooded with sunshine from morning till night. An electric reading lamp by his bed relieved many sleepless hours. He often contrasted the comforts of this house with the wretched, sunless, mudbrick dwelling of his early days in Senneh.

Hardly a year of relative quiet had been enjoyed in the new home when Rebka was taken ill. As her sickness dragged on for months and hope of recovery grew dim, her one wish was once more to see Samuel, who was spending his leave with his family in America. Upon his return she thrilled to hear everything about his wife and children and about his trip. She showed a keen interest in news of the war,[3] which had now started.

During this time her life-partner of over fifty years bore up wonderfully well but on the last day he knew the

[3]World War II.

end was near. His heartache made the grief of the others more poignant, especially when they heard his quiet sobbing as he left the sickroom.

The end came on November 18, 1939. She passed away very quietly, her closing eyes comforted by the sight of her children, grandchildren and two great-grandchildren. The funeral took place in the Mission church, conducted by Dr. Schuler of the American Mission and the Rev. Jollynous Hakim, an Iranian clergyman of the Church of England. Hundreds of people were present, from Cabinet ministers to beggars, from many races and creeds.

For some months after the death of her mother Sarah remained in Teheran to care for her father. When home duties necessitated her return to Hamadan, her oldest daughter, Nectar, volunteered to take her place. Her two little children helped to brighten the atmosphere of the home.

Less than four months after Rebka's passing came word of Kaka's death.

Meanwhile World War II spread its gloom over everything. Samuel was planning to return to America to make his home there with his wife and children. As Dr. Sa'eed saw his loved ones departing one by one, he felt a deep sense of loneliness. Increasing deafness made conversation difficult and robbed him of the pleasure of listening to the prattle of the two little great-grandchildren.

In the quietness of his bedroom at night through hours of sleeplessness he turned his thoughts heavenward and longed for the call to go. So in the loneliness of his last years he learned more deeply the all-sufficiency and sustaining love of God. With the increasing failure of his physical powers there was an ever quickening of the spiritual. As the war spread, casting its sense of depression over the entire world, his soul rested more completely in "the peace of God which passeth all understanding."[4]

----
[4]Phil. 4:7

The twilight of his life was not darkened by any clouds of doubt or anxiety. The light of heaven shone on his pilgrim pathway with an ever-increasing brilliance. He belonged more to the world beyond than to earth.

On June 1, 1942 Dr. Sa'eed quietly passed his seventy-ninth milestone. Besides Samuel all of Sarah's four children and her two grandchildren were present in Teheran to celebrate the birthday. It was both a reunion and farewell, for in a few days Samuel would be leaving for the south on his way to America. The doctor decided to synchronize his departure for Hamadan for the summer with that of Samuel.

On the 4th of June, Dr. Sa'eed's wedding anniversary, the last things were packed into bags. He expressed concern over the dangers of travel in war time, but he said to Samuel: "I am glad, however, that the way was opened for you to reunite with your family. I shall be anxious until I hear of your safe arrival. Send me a cablegram as soon as you can."

At the gate a number of people had gathered — some acquaintances, others from curiosity, including the beggars who always seem to sprout out of the ground at any departure scene, hoping to collect a few coins as life insurance for a safe journey. The car that was to take Samuel to the railroad station was to return to take his father to Hamadan. After saying good-bye to the others, Samuel turned to his father for what he knew would be their last farewell. In the quaint manner practised on their many partings Dr. Sa'eed slowly put out the little finger of his right hand. Just as cautiously, with his right forefinger and thumb Samuel took his father's finger tip and gave it a loving squeeze. Then he stepped into the car and was gone.

In the restful atmosphere of the Hamadan garden Dr. Sa'eed soon plunged into his never-ending studies with a rare sense of satisfaction. He was now engaged in writing another book. He seldom went to the city, but a number of friends had access to him. The ability to give himself undividedly to his task kept him mentally occupied and happy, but sometimes in the evening he would say, "Still no news from Samuel. I wonder where he is held up."

Forty anxious days passed. He was seated on the terrace, writing as usual, with his books around him, when the message was handed to him. His face lighted up with joy as he called out, "A cablegram from Samuel! He has arrived safely. I am relieved and happy now."

Two weeks passed. It was the 29th day of July. At the breakfast table the doctor seemed weary and drawn in the face.

"You look tired, Papa. Is anything wrong?" Sarah asked most solicitously.

"Nothing serious, thank you. I had a bad night."

He picked up his books and writing materials to seek out his favorite haunt on the terrace. Then off he went for his morning walk. Half an hour later he returned, feeling sharp, cutting pains that came in ever-increasing intensity. He called his grandson at once: "Willie dear, run to the American hospital and get me a stretcher as fast as you can. No time must be wasted."

William ran for all he was worth to cover the distance of more than a mile to the hospital, only to find that the doctor in charge was at the clinic another mile away. There he found Dr. Packard, who offered to drive out to the garden to bring Dr. Sa'eed into the hospital in his car, but William was sure that he could not stand the jolting. So Dr. Packard returned to the hospital to prepare for an emergency operation while William went back to the garden with the stretcher.

Dr. Sa'eed was put on the stretcher and two servants carried him. Sarah and her two daughters then in Hamadan walked to the edge of the garden, where they kissed him in farewell. It was two o'clock when they reached the hospital. He was still conscious, but his strength was rapidly ebbing. Spinal anasthesia was given at once, which brought complete relief from the pain, but the successful outcome of surgical intervention now seemed highly doubtful, especially in view of his advanced age. However, it was decided to attempt it.

While Dr. Packard was scrubbing up in preparation for the operation, Dr. Tatevos arrived and was told to go into the operating room to see his father-in-law. He returned at once, saying the patient had no pulse. Together the doctors rushed in, to find the end was near. At five o'clock he passed away without regaining consciousness.

The funeral took place the next morning in the beautiful chapel which Mr. Hawkes had built in the Protestant cemetery in memory of his wife. The chapel and grounds were thronged with men and women of many nationalities and creeds. The Rev. H. C. Gurney of the Church Missionary Society in Isfahan, who was spending his vacation in Hamadan, conducted the service, at which other friends paid their loving tribute. One of Dr. Sa'eed's own hymns[5] was sung, a hymn whose every line is a testimony to the perfections of Christ by a soul thoroughly captivated thereby.

Interment took place under a large walnut tree in front of the chapel, next to the graves of Mr. and Mrs. Hawkes, his early missionary pupils in the Persian language and his lifelong friends. The simple tombstones there bear silent witness to three lives dedicated to the service of God in Iran.

And so came the fulfilment of that hymn[6] Dr. Sa'eed so much loved:

> *In the radiance of the glory*
> *First I saw His blessed Face,*
> *And for ever shall that glory*
> *Be my home, my dwelling-place.*

---

[5]See page 188
[6]"Beyond the Brightness of the Sun," by Mrs. Frances Bevan

Translation of
DR. SA'EED'S HYMN

Christ is my Life, and Christ is my Light;
Christ is my Guide in the darkness of night;
Priest and strong Advocate Christ is for me;
Christ is my Master, to truth he's the key.

Christ is my Leader, he peace to me brought;
Christ is my Savior, Christ righteousness wrought;
Christ is my Prophet, my Priest, and my King;
My Way, and the Truth to which firmly I cling.

Christ is my Glory, and Christ is my Crown;
Christ shares my troubles when woe strikes me
   down;
Christ is my Treasure in heaven above;
In every deep sorrow he soothes me with love.

Christ is my Savior, my Portion, my Lord;
All honor and homage to Him I accord.
Christ is my Peace, and Christ my Repast;
Christ is my Rapture forever to last.

In joy and in sorrow Christ satisfies me;
'Tis Christ who from bondage of sin set me free.
In all times of sickness Christ is my Health;
In want and in poverty Christ is my Wealth.

Dr. Sa'eed's Grave in Hamadan